BFI TV Classics

BFI TV Classics is a series of books celebrating key individual television programmes and series. Television scholars, critics and novelists provide critical readings underpinned with careful research, alongside a personal response to the programme and a case for its 'classic' status.

The
League of
Gentlemen

Leon
Hunt

palgrave
macmillan

A BFI book published by Palgrave Macmillan

First published in 2008 by
PALGRAVE MACMILLAN
Houndmills, Basingstoke, Hampshire RG21 6XS and
175 Fifth Avenue, New York, N.Y. 10010
Companies and Representatives throughout the world

on behalf of the

BRITISH FILM INSTITUTE
21 Stephen Street, London W1T 1LN
<www.bfii.org.uk>

There's more to discover about fiilm and television through the BFI. Our
world-renowned archive, cinemas, festivals, fiilms, publications and learning
resources are here to inspire you.

PALGRAVE MACMILLAN is the global academic imprint of the Palgrave Macmillan
division of St. Martin's Press, LLC and of Palgrave Macmillan Ltd.
Macmillan® is a registered trademark in the United States, United Kingdom
and other countries. Palgrave is a registered trademark in the European Union and other countries.

Images from *The League of Gentlemen*, BBC.

None of the content of this publication is intended to imply that it is endorsed by the
programme's broadcaster or production companies involved.

Set by Cambrian Typesetters, Camberley, Surrey
Printed in China

This book is printed on paper suitable for recycling and made from fully
managed and sustained forest sources. Logging, pulping and manufacturing
processes are expected to conform to the environmental regulations of the
country of origin.

British Library Cataloguing-in-Publication Data
A catalogue record for this book is available from the British Library

ISBN 978–1–84457–269–4

Contents

Acknowledgments vi

1 The Gentlemen 1
2 Special Stuff 16
3 Local 39
4 Pandemonium Carnival 75
5 Follow the Red Bag 105

Postscript: Escape from Royston Vasey? 131

Notes 134
Select Bibliography 140
Credits 143
Index 148

Acknowledgments

Many thanks to Jeremy Dyson and Mark Gatiss. Thanks also to Karl Schmid at PBJ Management. Susy Campanale and Milly Williamson read draft chapters of this book and I am grateful for their comments, suggestions and encouragement. I had several fruitful conversations with Peter Hutchings about *The League of Gentlemen* and he provided me with a draft of his essay on the series. Chapter 4 was adapted into a research paper at Roehampton University (under the more scholarly sounding title 'The Local and the Uncanny'); thanks to Paul Bowman for inviting me and to Stacey Abbott for being such an excellent respondent. I am also grateful to Rebecca Barden and the readers on the BFI editorial board for their input, all of which strengthened the manuscript. Brunel University provided me with study leave to complete the manuscript, and I particularly appreciate the support of Julian Petley.

This book is dedicated to Chica – copy-editing maestro, comedy connoisseur, survivor of Pauline's vicious tongue.

1 The Gentlemen

As BBC2 revved up for its spring season in 1999, it began to show trailers for a comedy series that, hyperbole aside, looked like nothing else on television. Grotesque characters delivered lines not yet classifiable as catchphrases, but already sufficiently insidious to burrow into the unconscious, waiting to be repeated in workplaces and playgrounds. What was less clear was whether it was a sitcom or a sketch show, a question to which the series did not provide a conclusive answer when it was broadcast. *The League of Gentlemen* would often appear to be other things too, not least blackly comic horror. The phrase 'northern Gothic' was widely applied to the series, set in a provincial location on the border between town and (bleak) countryside and populated by a gallery of strange characters, some of whom would command enormous affection from audiences. A prim middle-class family obsessed with toads and hygiene subjected their nephew to an impossibly inflexible domestic regime. The restart officer at the unemployment office systematically demoralised the 'dole scum' in her care. A sinister butcher supplied a mysterious addictive substance to an elite clientele. A travelling circus arrived in town, presided over by a nightmarish figure with a disturbing interest in other people's wives. Above all, there was the Local Shop run by a misshapen couple, simultaneously sibling and spouse to one another, prepared to go to extremes to keep the town free of outsiders. Welcome to Royston Vasey.

Critically celebrated at the time, showered with awards, an enduring reference point for innovative British comedy series, *The*

League of Gentlemen has been bafflingly neglected as an object of more
sustained analysis. It is the aim of this book to rectify that neglect and to
explore this richly fascinating series in greater critical depth. *The League
of Gentlemen* was a sketch show that played less and less like a sketch
show, until it ceased to be one altogether. Its three lead performers were
so versatile and physically mutable that the *Radio Times* provided a
chart to help the audience recognise who played who among the huge
cast of characters.[1] It was 'dark', a word that became almost as
umbilically linked to the series as the word 'Local'; some of this
'darkness' derived from the horror genre, some of it from elements of
tragedy, cruelty and 'bad taste'. It was 'northern', a more contentious
claim than might first appear, although international sales suggest that
its representation of the 'Local' was translatable to those with no
experience of the English north–south divide. It was a cult show, but it
spawned a multitude of catchphrases, often a sign of mainstream,
audience-uniting aspirations. It made many fan-pleasing references to
film and television, while simultaneously appearing unique and original,
creating a 'world' that its followers felt able to inhabit. It was an awards
magnet, at least initially, but alienated and lost some viewers as it tried
new things or became even darker. It depicted a grim, ugly town, but
raised the bar for the look of British comedy series, with a richness of
design detail unprecedented in live-action TV comedy. It was set in a
town named after an offensive comedian, who later appeared as its
mayor. It (probably) paved the way for *Little Britain* (BBC3/BBC2/
BBC1, 2003–), which achieved greater mainstream success but had to
endure persistent accusations that it was *League*-lite. Listing the series'
salient features in this way also indicates that it does not lend itself to a
single, unified approach. Sketch shows are scattershot in nature, even
those with a unified setting like this one, which is possibly a way of
gently breaking it to the reader that my approach will be scattershot too.
Nevertheless, certain themes and concerns predominate throughout my
analysis: the regional identity of the series and its sense of place, its
mixing of comedy and horror, its intertextual complexity, its cult status
and its willingness to experiment with what was already a relatively

2

unusual format, sometimes to the detriment of its popularity. I write from what is starting to be seen as a hybrid critical identity, the academic-fan. On the one hand, aspects of the series have resonated with my familiarity with certain types of academic theory. On the other hand, I am a fan of the show, and in discussions of comedy, personal taste has a tendency to elbow its way to the front. In other words, I make little attempt to disguise my investment in convincing the reader that *The League of Gentlemen* is as great as I think it is, but without losing sight of some of the more contentious aspects of the series. Different sections of the book place an emphasis on different critical approaches, some more theoretical, some more evaluative, and with an occasional indulgent excursion into transparent celebration.

Just as we make a distinction between *Monty Python's Flying Circus* (a TV series, BBC2, 1969–74) and Monty Python (a team, a brand name), I shall speak of both *The League of Gentlemen* and the League of Gentlemen (keep an eye on those italics). More often, I shall refer to 'the League' or 'the Gents', as a rough equivalent to the informal 'Python' or 'the Pythons'. The focus of this introductory chapter is particularly on 'the League', both the pre-history of the TV series and how the team appears to have functioned *as* a team. For viewers who first encountered the League of Gentlemen on television, they seemed to have sprung from nowhere fully formed, with no visible connection to existing TV comedy networks, but the basis for the series had been gestating in fringe theatre and then on radio since 1994.

The League of Gentlemen consists of Jeremy Dyson, Mark Gatiss, Steve Pemberton and Reece Shearsmith. The latter three play the vast majority of the characters between them, in addition to writing the series with Dyson, whose onscreen appearances are confined to cameos; look out for him buying cigarette lighters from Les McQueen, playing rhythm guitar with Creme Brulee or heckling Geoff Tipps during his stand-up act. From 1986–9, Gatiss and Pemberton studied Theatre Arts at Bretton Hall, a college of art, music and drama affiliated to (and later merged with) Leeds University; Shearsmith was in the year below. Gatiss plays Royston Vasey's demon butcher Hilary Briss, hapless vet Dr

Chinnery, and Creme Brulee's erstwhile guitarist Les McQueen alongside
numerous other roles. Hilary apart, his most characteristic roles are often
innocents like Chinnery, Les and hotelier Alvin. 'They're kind of
well-meaning, kind-hearted people and life has dealt them a bad hand', he
says. 'Les isn't a bitter man at all, but there's a wonderful self-delusion
going on and Alvin is the same.'[2] But Gatiss is arguably at his best in two
stand-alone monologues, as a depressed cave guide with a guilty memory
and a sinister mortician. As his novels about bisexual spy Lucifer Box and
his work on *Doctor Who* (BBC, 1963–89, BBC1, 2005–) suggest,[3] Gatiss
has a fondness for period. 'I would say that I have a facility for historical
comedy, and a sort of bleakness in my soul which leads me down the path
of those sort of semi-tragic characters – that's what I do.'[4] While *The
League of Gentlemen* ostensibly offers few outlets for this, 'The Curse of
Karrit Poor', the third story in the Christmas Special (2000), has Gatiss all
over it. Pemberton collaborated with Gatiss on a number of projects both
at Bretton Hall and after: a spoof working men's club act (Fat and Crass),
a game-show parody *Damage Your Children*, and a comic play about two
hitmen contracted to kill death (*Death Warmed Up*). Pemberton's
signature roles are two of the series' most popular characters, Tubbs and
Pauline. He brings an energy and warmth to seemingly monstrous
characters, but can play more purely terrifying figures like Pop. While the
word 'androgynous' does not spring to mind, he is for some reason the
most convincing Gent in drag. Pemberton is an extraordinary physical
performer. Witness him donning carpet-restoring shoes as Harvey Denton
and transforming into some kind of peculiar self-satisfied cyborg crossed
with a slow-motion ice-skater. This might be what Henri Bergson had in
mind in his influential essay on humour when he equated physical
comedy with the human body's resemblance to a machine.[5] Shearsmith
began to collaborate with Pemberton, including a comic play that
featured the first appearance of Pauline Campbell-Jones, a character
based on Shearsmith's own restart officer during a period of
unemployment. His two most popular characters are Edward and Papa
Lazarou, but his particular speciality as an actor is impotent rage; the
businessman Geoff Tipps and Legz Akimbo Theatre Company's

4

writer-director Ollie Plimsolls, Shearsmith is most recognisable as
Benjamin, but he is also the Gent who most 'disappears' into his make-up.
It may take a while for first-time viewers to work out that Ross, Geoff,
Edward and Papa Lazarou are all played by the same person; when Papa
terrorises Bernice at the climax of the Christmas Special, it barely registers
that Shearsmith is effectively chasing himself. Dyson is the only member
of the League who did not attend Bretton Hall. Instead, he studied
Philosophy at Leeds University itself, going on to do a Masters in
Screenwriting at the Northern School of Film and Television. He
performed in the first shows staged by what would become the League of
Gentlemen. In a different kind of sketch show, one might speculate that he
might have continued to do so; the Python team, for example, possessed
varying levels of acting ability. After the League's early performances,
however, it became apparent that the character-based material required
the high-level acting skills that Dyson's three friends possessed:

> The three of them were very strong on stagecraft. They were quite snobby
> about it, even in those very first shows. They hated things that were shoddy. 5
> It all dated back to their time at Bretton because they took a pride in what
> they did. I was floored by what they did because it would just come
> naturally to them, it would just flow out of them. All three of them had a
> genius.[6]

As the non-actor of the group, Dyson has sometimes seemed
vulnerable to being marginalised by critics understandably seduced by
the performative aspects of the series, and some of this seems to have
been felt by the writer; 'because I was a non-performer, there was a
period where I was self-conscious about that and felt that I had to pedal
harder to justify my place in the pecking order'. In Ben Thompson's
book on post-alternative comedy, the chapter on the League is headed
'Three character actors no longer in search of an author' and provides a
narrative in which the three performers write material to showcase their
virtuosity in a way that would not otherwise have been possible if
working solely as actors-for-hire. There is doubtless no ill will here, but

it does make it sound as though there are only *three* (significant) Gentlemen, an impression exacerbated by his referring to Dyson as 'Ringo'.[7] In any case, Dyson has been assistant producer since series two and is an acclaimed writer in his own right.

Like Monty Python before them, the League members write mainly in pairs. Where Gatiss plays the lead character (Chinnery, Les, Alvin, Hilary, Lance) he generally co-writes with Dyson. Together they also write the hygiene-obsessed Dentons, Judee and Iris, and Pop. Pemberton and Shearsmith are the creators of Tubbs and Edward, Pauline, Geoff Tipps, Papa Lazarou, and Charlie and Stella. Python's creative partnerships often have authorial quirks attributed to them, John Cleese and Graham Chapman associated with vitriol and cruelty (and dead parrots), Michael Palin and Terry Jones with surreal 'silliness' like 'The Spanish Inquisition'. There are discernible differences between the paired Gents, but they don't lend themselves to such a schematic opposition. Les, Chinnery and Alvin are gentler characters, but anyone discerning a 'softer' side to the Dyson–Gatiss partnership might want to check out Pop, Hilary and Lance before leaping to conclusions. There is an immediacy about Pemberton and Shearsmith's material that might explain why they created so many of the show's catchphrases; their ear for the absurdity of overheard phrases or out-of-context film and TV dialogue resonated through the series' popular reception. 'They were always reading things out that were so instantaneously funny that it was a joy to listen to', remembers Gatiss, feeling that his and Dyson's material didn't always get the same reaction at read-throughs. 'I always envied them their fluency and their genius', says Dyson.

> I remember watching them perform 'Mau Mau' for the first time in their front room down the road when we were living in Highgate and thinking 'You *bastards*!' Because you just knew it was a classic you were watching. You just knew that that was better than a Python sketch.

Pemberton and Shearsmith often trade in the 'traps' of socially realist British comedy. Frustrated joke-teller Geoff and warring couple

Charlie and Stella in particular belong to a tradition that includes
Hancock, Harold Steptoe and Basil Fawlty, characters who long for
something better, or to *be* something better, but will forever remain
confined by a relationship, job or living arrangement, but most cruelly
of all, by their own limitations. British sitcom loves its losers, especially
those with frustrated aspirations, and the 'classics' often develop this to
a level that knocks on the door of 'proper' drama. Both teams offer
characters defined by disappointment, but if Geoff is a bitter, angry
character, Les retains a misplaced optimism that dooms him to an
eternity of crumpled ambition. He will never rejoin his band Creme
Brulee or recapture their also-ran 'fame', but he will never be able to let
them go. Dyson and Gatiss have a strong narrative sense, as
accomplished storytellers in other media, and their humour often seems
less gag-based, the 'Special Stuff' served by Hilary Briss being a case in
point. 'I suppose, with Jeremy and I, it's sort of a slower burn', says
Gatiss. Both fans of Alan Bennett, they share his ability to hint at
unspoken tragedy and horror, never more so than in their cave guide
haunted by the death of a young boy; if 'Mau Mau' is (as Dyson claims)
'better than a Python sketch', then 'Stumphole Cavern' is their 'Mau
Mau'. It's tempting to suggest that Shearsmith and Pemberton represent
the populist side of the League, the road that leads to *Little Britain* and
Catherine Tate, while Dyson and Gatiss epitomise its cultishness, but
even that is too neat. Chinnery is as simple and populist as could be,
while who would have guessed that a character as seemingly obscure as
Papa Lazarou would become so iconic? Like Python, the League
includes one gay member (Chapman and Gatiss respectively), but it's
interesting that the 'queerer' material, like Herr Lipp and transsexual
Barbara, is usually written by Pemberton and Shearsmith. They have
sometimes written in other combinations: Gatiss with Pemberton,
Dyson with Shearsmith, or solo, as Eric Idle did in Python. Dyson
initially created Pop, Les, Lance and the Dentons alone, subsequently
co-writing them with Gatiss. Shearsmith wrote Chris Frost, the
embittered store detective ('Chalk it up') who makes a one-off
appearance in series two, while Gatiss wrote mortician Owen

Fallowfield for the League's 1996 residency at the Canal Café in London and later revived him for series three.

The League's world grew out of two sets of influences. On the one hand, their cult status is inseparable from the film and TV references that proliferate in their work. As Jeremy Dyson once put it: 'we began to find that we were the living disproof of every criticism our parents and teachers had slung at us – it was precisely because we'd watched so much television that we were beginning to succeed'.[8] This has given the League a very particular place in British culture, as both curators of popular culture and creators of a TV series that has already left its mark on popular memory. But they have largely managed to be more than the sum of their intertexts because there is also an element of 'real life' in the series. They often cite Alan Bennett and Victoria Wood as influences, influences that manifest themselves not through imitation but through an attentiveness to the humour in everyday speech and behaviour. Some of this everyday life was encountered directly, through encounters with eccentric landlords, wary shopkeepers and silvery hoteliers with glamorous wives. But just as much was extracted from the mediated 'reality' of daytime and reality TV, or documentaries about gender realignment.

Bretton Hall's alumnae include Colin Welland, Kay Mellor, Richard O'Brien, John Godber and Mark Thomas. In 2004, the college was deemed no longer financially viable, and its students moved to Leeds University campus in 2007. In an episode of Radio 4's *Front Row* celebrating the institution (3 May 2007), Gatiss and Pemberton struck a discordant note at the wake: 'We laughed' was Pemberton's mischievous response to its impending closure and the League members have never disguised their antipathy to the Theatre Arts course. The educational theatre group Legz Akimbo, whose would-be progressive plays about disability and sexuality fail to mask toe-curling condescension and ignorance, can be seen as a revenge on Bretton Hall. Nevertheless, the college occupies an important place in the team's formation; two other Bretton students would play key roles in what became the League of Gentlemen. Gordon Anderson (then Gordon Scott) had left Bretton Hall for Leeds University, where he befriended Dyson. Anderson not only co-founded 606 Theatre with Pemberton, but introduced Dyson to Gatiss, to some initial resistance until an enduring friendship grew out of shared obsessions. Dyson recalls this meeting of minds and tastes:

> I'd thought that these passions were completely private, and it was me who had this bizarre mixture of things, and to suddenly meet somebody who had almost the identical bizarre mixture of things that had developed for him independently was an amazing affirmation. It was *so* specific that (Mark) loved the dust jacket on the *Monty Python Bok* as much as I did, simultaneously loving (*Doctor Who* story) 'The Talons of Weng Chiang', simultaneously loving *Blood on Satan's Claw*. It was like winning the lottery that you could find somebody who had these things that were so disparate and yet so much aligned.

Simon Messingham, currently one half of comedy team Kirk and Messingham, was in the year above and worked with Gatiss and Pemberton on *Death Warmed Up*, among other things. Like Gatiss, he was a *Doctor Who* fan who would later write novels during that series' 'wilderness years'. At the end of 1994 and into 1995, he was (briefly) a 'Gentleman' in all but name when Anderson brought the five of them together to stage a sketch show called *This Is It!*. Gatiss remembers how it came about:

> There was this festival called 'I Wish I'd Seen That' and the idea was to re-stage fringe shows that had gone down very well but hadn't had a very wide public at the Cockpit Theatre just off the Edgware Road. For one reason or another, (Anderson) had a five-night slot but no play. And Gordon approached me and Steve and Simon and Reece and Jeremy.

All five would perform in *This Is it!* 'What's remarkable about that show', says Dyson, 'is how much of it went on to be in the series.' Bernice (played by Dyson, 'the one thing I *could* do, actually') and Pauline were in the show, as was Geoff, at that time one of five

9

businessmen. An incompetent medium Mr Asmodeus did an act that would later be adopted by Papa Lazarou. Mr McCunn, a vicious PE teacher played by Gatiss, would become a stage regular but, in spite of a brief radio cameo, never made it to the TV series. Other material from *This Is It!* was unsuited to the unified town setting that would later distinguish the League, although some would resurface in the touring *Local Show for Local People* (2000–1), like two audience members at *Hamlet* who behave like football fans. Another featured earnest academics debating the politics of boy bands using gay imagery to sell records before, as Gatiss describes it, 'they just descend into these giggly queens', each declaring Robbie Williams to be his favourite. The show featured film and TV spoofs, including a spin on *Prime Suspect* (Granada/ITV, 1991–2006). As in subsequent pre-TV shows and the first half of the *Local Show*, the nascent Gents donned tuxedoes, but also plastered on make-up; 'it just *ran*, like Dirk Bogarde in *Death in Venice*', laughs Gatiss.

Finding the right arena for the emerging show was not always easy. 'We did a couple of gigs, one in King's Cross, and it was like a stand-up show', recalls Gatiss.

> We had a ten-minute slot and it just died a death. It started well because we were doing direct address stuff, but in any sketch people were talking and we quickly realised we needed our own night where all the rules are set by you.

One such night, or rather four, took place at the Komedia Theatre in Brighton in September 1995. Messingham had moved on,[9] Dyson was no longer performing, and the resulting division of labour now had a name. Other titles like 'The Porn Dwarves' and 'The Assassination Bureau' were mooted, but Gatiss's suggestion was the winner:

> At that stage I didn't realise that 'The League of Gentlemen' had been used by Robert Fripp as a prog rock group. It was the original name of the followers of the Scarlet Pimpernel, which is where it comes from, and to me it was just a lovely old film.[10] I thought, 'That rather suits' and of course everything went from there. I thought, 'Wouldn't it be nice if we looked like a very old-fashioned revue group but we were anything but, we were actually rather nasty?'

Brighton would yield another important part of the League's world.
On a day trip to Rottingdean, a suspicious local shopkeeper would plant
a seed that would grow into the series' two most widely recognised
characters.

At the end of 1995, the League staged a show at the Tristram
Bates Theatre in Covent Garden, expressly to attract notorious comedy
management company Avalon. The League's drag-heavy repertoire was
possibly not what macho Avalon was looking for, and the Gents would
later sign with the quirkier PBJ, home of Reeves and Mortimer, Eddie
Izzard, Rowan Atkinson and Chris Morris. A key turning point would
come in April 1996, when they began the first of two residencies at the
Canal Café in London, performing every Monday night. With a growing
gallery of characters (the Dentons and Herr Lipp emerged at the Canal
Café), they hit on a strategy for getting audiences to come back, as
Gatiss explains:

> we had this whole rolling schedule thing of changing a sketch or two a
> week, so that at the end of the month it was a new show. We did a
> three-month residency, which gave us loads of material, but it also meant if
> people wanted to come again four weeks later they'd effectively have a
> whole new show to see.

11

'Never the same show twice!' claimed the posters. There was, in Dyson's
words, 'an element of expediency' in this approach, but it often took the
form of an increasing element of seriality. 'Because we were getting
people coming back, it seemed only logical, I suppose, to write
instalments, serials', confirms Gatiss. They even brought some of the
storylines to a close, he recalls:

> Mr McCunn had a huge breakdown, Pauline stabbed Ross in the eye. The
> Dentons ended with Benjamin being changed into a toad. The local shop
> ended with me as Lord Local, basically Lord Summerisle (from *The Wicker
> Man*), coming in. They were six-parters, I suppose.

The League made their first appearance at the Edinburgh Festival in 1996. When they returned the following year, they would win the Perrier Award, the first sketch show to do so since Cambridge Footlights in 1981.[11] The Perrier had lost some of its cultural capital in the 1980s, scorned by the 'alternative' comedians of the era, but it had begun to mean something again in the 1990s. Dyson attributes this to Steve Coogan winning it in 1992, even though his emergence seemed a mixed blessing for the League. 'I remember Mark ringing me when (Coogan's character) Paul Calf first went out and he said, "That's it, we've missed the boat." You know, we were fucked – he's gone and done it!' Coogan represented what they were aiming for themselves, 'that fusion of brilliantly naturalistic performance fused with the British Vaudeville and Variety elements that we also loved'. Coogan seemed like a contemporary manifestation of the kind of performers the three actors in the League aspired to, such as Leonard Rossiter, Alec Guinness, Alastair Sim and Ronnie Barker, actors who specialised in comedy, rather than comedians. He had even anticipated the use of a unifying town, Ottle, for the six characters he would play in the otherwise self-contained episodes of *Coogan's Run* (BBC2, 1995).

Edinburgh 1997 won the League the Perrier, but Edinburgh 1996 had already won them a radio series. Producer Sarah Smith had come to see them, and would play a major role in honing the version of the League that would appear on television. As producer, director and script editor, Smith has retained an association with 'dark' or controversial comedy. She would go on to work on the notorious *Brass Eye Special* (Channel 4, 2001) that satirised the media's sensationalisation of paedophilia, and produced *Nighty Night* (BBC3, 2004–5). Gatiss characterises the relationship as 'combative' but 'fruitful', with many 'lively debates' about what the show would be. Dyson confirms that she

> had a kind of clear grasp of what the thing was at the heart of what we did that was different from what other people did. That was really the process over those three years, from '94 through to the radio series, a gradual weeding out of the kind of stuff that other people might have done.

The League have always worn their influences on their collective sleeve, but by the time of their first TV series, to say that they were unique was more than hype because a lot of work had gone into ensuring that that was the case. Smith was particularly keen for them to place all their characters in the same town as they transferred to broadcast media, 'Spent' on the radio and 'Royston Vasey' on TV. She was producer and script editor of the radio series and the first television series before handing over to Jemma Rodgers. *On the Town with The League of Gentlemen* was broadcast on Radio 4 from 6 November to 11 December 1997 and would win them their second award, the Sony Silver. It would not be their last trophy; BAFTAs (Best Comedy Series, Best Costume Design), Royal Television Society Awards (Best Entertainment Series, Best Costume, Best Production Design, Best Title Music) and the Golden Rose of Montreux would follow after the TV series was broadcast. Even series three, which received a more divided reception, won the *South Bank Show* Comedy Award.

In the buildup to their first series, the League used their 'fringe' origins one last time. The radio series had added a few new characters, of whom Dr Chinnery would be particularly important. In a series of shows at the Gatehouse Theatre in Highgate, they tried out some new characters created for the TV series; Pop, Les McQueen and Papa Lazarou, who would not start abducting wives until series two.

If Sarah Smith played a crucial role in helping shape *The League of Gentlemen* for radio and then television, several other collaborators played important roles in the TV series and remained constant members of the creative team. Director Steve Bendelack had a particularly distinguished track record in TV comedy (*Spitting Image* [ITV, 1984–96], *The Royle Family* [BBC1, 1998–2000], *Little Britain*), and would also direct their film and post-TV live shows.[12] Other important contributors were production designer Grenville Horner, whose assistant Sarah Kane was credited as art director from the Christmas Special onwards, costume designer Yves Barre and director of photography Rob Kitzmann. Joby Talbot has been the League's regular composer since series one. Positioned somewhere between pop (his work with the Divine Comedy) and modern classical (Classic FM

13

Composer in Residence), Talbot was not an obvious candidate to create 'comedy' music, but scored to the Gothic, melodramatic and even unexpectedly poignant qualities in the series. The Christmas Special alone features about thirty minutes of original music and is possibly the high point of their collaboration. One of his most beautiful pieces was the subject of some controversy when the final episode of series three was transmitted on BBC2, the elegiac end-title music notoriously ruined by an announcer and an early example of 'credit-squeezing'. 'I went *apoplectic*,' Gatiss recalls.

> I rang Jon Plowman. I was crying because of course we had actually spoken a lot beforehand to (the BBC trailer department) and I said, 'This may well be the end, this beautiful piece of music. Can we treasure, for once, the moment of transmission?' And they said 'Yes', and then they fucking talked over it!

After presenting their characters in tuxedoes on stage and then on radio, the Gents had to fix the look of their characters for television. While the make-up designs were simpler in execution than they might have seemed (a full latex head in series three was abandoned), they did become an essential part of *The League of Gentlemen* and a progression from the sellotape used to push up Tubbs and Edward's noses on stage. One might therefore expect an 'authorial' figure comparable to Horner or Barre to have handled make-up on the series. Instead, the job changed hands several times, always with input from the Gents themselves, as Gatiss explains:

> We did a forty minute version of episode 1 in the July of 1998, and then we began shooting the rest of it in the autumn, after [BBC2 controller] Mark Thompson said yes. That pilot was set up by Helen Barrett in cahoots with us, and our drawings and our suggestions kind of set the look of the characters. So when Vanessa White came in to do the series, it was essentially carrying that on, and then after two years, for the Special, we moved to Daniel Phillips, and then for the third series, his assistant [Diane Chenery-Wickens].

Another distinguished name on the credits took a more
hands-off role. Jon Plowman, BBC's Head of Comedy from 1994 to
2007, was executive producer on the series. '(He) would routinely turn
up with a sheaf of notes two days before transmission and we'd just go
"It's too late!"' laughs Gatiss.

Having provided an overview of the League of Gentlemen as a
team and an evolving enterprise that would form the basis of the TV
series, it is time to turn our attention more directly to that series. 'Special
Stuff' examines *The League of Gentlemen*'s cult credentials, placing it in
the context of 'alternative' comedy on TV but also considering less
overtly comic qualities, such as its 'darkness' and its creation of a
'world'. 'Local' focuses particularly on series one and two, which draw
mainly on material developed in the live shows but incorporate it into
loose story arcs. It also considers the series' sense of place and its
regional identity. 'Pandemonium Carnival' looks at the Gothic aspects
of the series, with particular emphasis on the Christmas Special and the
figure of Papa Lazarou. The final chapter 'Follow the Red Bag' deals
with the third series, and is rather more evaluative in approach. While
series three's initial reception was mixed, with many regarding it as a
disappointment, its reputation has improved and re-evaluation seems
overdue. Our journey begins: Destination Royston Vasey. It goes
without saying that you'll never … well, you know.

15

2 Special Stuff

The 'classic' status of *The League of Gentlemen* cannot be separated from its 'cult' status. 'Classic' and 'cult' are not the same thing, of course, but nor are they unrelated – we commonly speak of 'cult classics' – particularly in comedy, where the 'alternative' is valued as a sign of innovation or pushing boundaries. When I proposed this volume for the TV Classics series, there was an interesting discussion about whether the programme *was* a classic. No one disputed its quality; there are awards and glowing reviews to support its excellence. But what does it mean to designate a niche-oriented TV show a 'classic', especially a recent one whose influence and long-term currency has yet to be established? The point of comparison offered, rightly, I think, was *Monty Python's Flying Circus*. I say 'rightly' because Python represents an enduring model for the 'cult comedy classic'.

It is widely accepted that *Monty Python* was a 'classic', flawed and inconsistent, but 'classic' nonetheless. But in what way? First, Python is regarded as innovative (even though sceptics might mention Spike Milligan here). Python experimented with the format of the sketch show; according to Terry Jones, 'We had the idea of a flow, one thing leading to another by association of ideas.'[13] If some of this was indebted to Milligan, Terry Gilliam's animations were startlingly original (as well as just plain startling.) Second, Python is considered to be influential, even though the nature of that influence is strangely intangible; as Sangster and Condon observe, the adjective 'Pythonesque' has 'evolved into a generic word for anything that isn't a traditional sitcom or purely linear narrative'.[14] The audience was small, the programme was broadcast in unenviable slots on what was then more of a minority channel than it is now. Moreover, we can often hear the studio audience not 'getting' the joke, lengthy silences accompanying some sketches. Roger Wilmut, noting the polite, subdued laughter that accompanied the now canonical 'Parrot sketch', remarks, 'It seems to be a characteristic of Python sketches that they do not make their greatest impact at first, but lie in the subconscious like a time-bomb.'[15] In other words, Python's 'classic status' was earned over time, but it was achieved through the currency of cult. In any case, claims to classic status are never objective. Canons are arbitrary, capricious and precarious, often determined by who shouts the loudest and gets others to join in (we *will* have trouble here.) So here's the pitch, and it's scarcely a controversial one. In an era already being celebrated as a 'Golden Age' for British TV comedy,[16] *The League of Gentlemen* is one of its greatest and most complete achievements. Although it stretches the parameters of the format, partly *because* it stretches it, it is arguably the best British sketch show of the last thirty years, more original and consistent than its nearest rival, *The Fast Show* (BBC2, 1994–2000). It became a journalistic cliché to head interviews and articles with the title 'In a League of its/their own' but, as hyperbole goes, this is among the more apposite.

17

   The League's ratings were respectable but modest, declining slightly during series two and dropping further for the Christmas Special and series three. The first series' ratings were comparable to *Bang Bang, It's Reeves and Mortimer* (BBC2, 1999), but lower than BBC2's most popular sitcom, *Gimme Gimme Gimme* (1999–2001), and considerably lower than repeats of *Red Dwarf* (BBC2, 1988–99).[17] The first episode of series two got the highest ratings *The League* ever enjoyed (3.07 million), but Papa Lazarou must have frightened some of those viewers away, given the subsequent drop. However, DVD sales have become an increasingly important arbiter of a TV series' more lasting status, and the League sold healthily. At one point, the series two video and DVD were the BBC's third biggest seller. As they toured their *Local Show for*

Local People in 2000–1, culminating in six weeks at the Theatre Royal, Drury Lane, and heard their catchphrases shouted from sold-out theatres, they were big in a way that ratings didn't reflect. The climactic residency was symbolic; the audience response on the LP *Monty Python Live at Drury Lane* (1974) confirms Python's transition from cult to classic.[18] *The League of Gentlemen* did not achieve the mainstream success of *Little Britain*, nor did it have quite the cultural impact of *The Office* (BBC2, 2001–3); as series three started to divide *The League*'s following, the second series of Ricky Gervais's sitcom was being celebrated as the *Fawlty Towers* (BBC2, 1975, 1979) of its day. However, *The League* left its mark on mainstream culture, and remains the most common point of comparison for dark comedy.

From Alternative to Cult

The phrase 'alternative comedy' arguably has two different usages. In its 'proper' sense, it refers to a specific movement (or moment) in British comedy, a generation of broadly oppositional comedians that came to prominence in the 1980s, leading to TV series like *The Young Ones* (BBC2, 1982–4) and *The Comic Strip Presents* (Channel 4, 1982–93, 1998, 2000, 2005.) But it is also applied to a longer tradition of comedy that is somehow positioned in opposition to a notional 'mainstream'. In the multichannel era, 'mainstream' comedy is harder to identify than it was in Monty Python's day. Few primetime sitcoms have quite the profile that *Little Britain* or *The Catherine Tate Show* (BBC2, 2004–) do. 'Mainstreams' are in any case abstract by nature, but their significance underlines the fact that the word 'alternative' is operating in a manner not dissimilar to 'cult'.

'Cult' implies something that is partly defined by its circulation and reception. Alternative comedy is associated with particular institutions, such as Footlights Revues (most of the Pythons, Fry and Laurie, Mitchell and Webb), the Comedy Store in Soho (many of the 1980s' comics), the Edinburgh Festival and Perrier Award. BBC Radio,

especially Radio 4, has a long history of comedy transitions to TV and
has more recently played an important role in establishing cult comedy
(*Dead Ringers* [BBC2, 2002], *Little Britain*, *The Mighty Boosh*).
The League's trajectory has become quite a familiar one, from
Edinburgh/Perrier Award to Radio 4 to BBC2 or 3. On TV, alternative
comedy could be seen as a sub-category of 'quality' TV, partly deriving
from a public- service ethos of innovation and diversity. The second
series of *The League of Gentlemen* was originally broadcast as part of
BBC2's Friday 'Comedy Night', but the channel was also repositioning
itself during this period under controller Jane Root. The target audience
would be older, more mainstream and suburban.[19] For series three, new
episodes of *The League of Gentlemen* premiered on BBC Choice directly
after BBC2's 10.00 pm broadcast of the preceding one. BBC Choice was
the digital channel that would pave the way for BBC3, which would
define its brash, youthful identity through 'new' comedy like *Little
Britain* and *The Mighty Boosh* (2004–).[20] One senses that the League's
'darkness' no longer fitted the 'new' BBC2 and, in paving the way for
Little Britain, they seemed to have unwittingly established the edgy
template for 'BBC3 comedy'. *Little Britain* made its TV debut on
BBC3's opening night and became the channel's biggest success to date,
progressing to BBC2 and then 1. Its first series was script edited by
Gatiss and directed by Steve Bendelack. One of its best characters,
mental hospital outpatient Anne, was created during improvisations
with Pemberton and Shearsmith. *Little Britain* shared the League's
vision of national insularity and stasis, best captured by Tom Baker's
narration: 'Britain, Britain, Britain, land of tradition, fish and fries.
The changing of the garden. Trooping the coloureds. But have you ever
wondered about the people of Britain? Nor have I.'

The similarity between Marjorie Dawes, bullying 'Fat Fighters'
matriarch, and Pauline was not lost on some reviewers, although both
belong to a longer tradition of comic monsters. *Little Britain* did not
lack distinctive comic creations of its own, like über-chav Vicky Pollard,
and could muster risk-taking material in its first series, like the teenage
boy sucking the toes of his best friend's elderly gran. But it is in many

19

ways a much more traditional sketch show than *The League of Gentlemen*, less interested in ongoing storylines and character development. While series two and three were no more repetitive than *The Fast Show*, Matt Lucas and David Walliams began to seem stretched thin as writers and there has been a sense of diminishing returns. Ratings and merchandising, however, tell another story.

The League have another connection to BBC3, whose controller Stuart Murphy formerly ran the digital channel UK Play/UKTV, which in 1999 obtained exclusive cable and satellite rights to the series. Lucas and Walliams would create *Rock Profiles* (1999) for the same channel. Nevertheless, if *The League of Gentlemen* can be seen as an influence on BBC3 comedy, when the BBC repeated all three series in 2006, it would be on the arts and culture digital channel BBC4. That decision sent out a mixed message about the corporation's later attitude towards the series: culturally significant, but strictly 'minority' in appeal.

Cult comedy often draws on other kinds of (non-comic) cultural capital. Python was filled with intellectual references, while the alternative comedy of the 80s drew on the politics and youth culture of the period. The cliché of comedy being 'the new rock'n'roll' can be traced at least as far back as Python being marketed as 'the Beatles of comedy' in the US by press agent Nancy Lewis.[21] More recently, comics like Russell Brand and Noel Fielding look more like rock stars than most rock stars do, and *The Mighty Boosh* has a strong subcultural vibe, from its pop references to its stylised music promo look. The League fit into more of a 'geek chic' aesthetic, from the dinner-jackets and Brylcreem of their early shows to the plethora of film and TV references; only Dyson looks as though he might be in a band (which he is).[22] The contemporaneous *Spaced* (Channel 4, 1999, 2001) – a postmodern flat-share sitcom, *Man about the House* (Thames Television, 1973–6) for the Tarantino generation – was even more referential than the League. Gatiss and Shearsmith both made cameo appearances in *Spaced*, but there are significant differences between the two shows. *Spaced* extends beyond film and TV, encompassing parodies of games like *Resident Evil* and *Tekken*, while its film references seem more indicative of a generation for whom cinema began with *Star Wars* (1977). It's hard to imagine the League 'doing' John Woo or *The Matrix* (1999), even though Gatiss played an Agent Smith-like character in *Spaced*. *The Shining* (1980) is about as contemporary as the League get, having cultivated a more retro and fogeyish demeanour.

In their history of alternative comedy, Wilmut and Rosengard define the term as both 'a rejection of the easy techniques of racist or sexist jokes on which so many mainstream television and club comics rely' and 'simply a rejection of the preceding fashions in comedy'.[23] We might identify three waves of alternative comedy in the second sense. First, there is the Oxbridge generation that includes the *Beyond the Fringe* team, the Pythons and *The Goodies* (BBC2/ITV, 1970–82); second, the actual 'alternative' comedians who largely distinguished themselves both from the 'mainstream' and the privileged backgrounds of the Footlights comedians. The third, 'post-alternative', wave, can be seen as starting from two points. The radio series *On the Hour* (Radio 4, 1991–2) would transfer to television as *The Day Today* (BBC2, 1994), a savage parody of TV news that saw some continuity with the satire of the Oxbridge tradition. The series propelled the careers of Armando Iannucci, Steve Coogan and Chris Morris, but Morris's kamikaze approach to taste and offence would make him a key figure in the 'Dark Comedy' to come. The other starting point is *Vic Reeves' Big Night Out* (Channel 4, 1990–1), a surreal, art-school reinvention of television variety for a young, cultish audience. Reeves was the catalyst for a lot of subsequent cult comedy, from the sublime (the League, *The Fast Show*, the first series of *Little Britain*, *The Mighty Boosh*) to the execrable (*Bo' Selecta!* [Channel 4, 2002–4], *Tittybangbang* [BBC3, 2005–]). Symptomatically, Reeves and his partner Bob Mortimer both rejected the politics of alternative comedy and rehabilitated comedy's connection to light entertainment and variety. Reeves was announced each week as 'Britain's top light entertainer and singer', even though it was difficult to determine the degree of irony in that title. The use of club comic Charlie Chuck in *The Smell of Reeves and Mortimer* (BBC2, 1993, 1995) left one uncertain whether Chuck was in on the joke. When the League cast

21

Roy 'Chubby' Brown as Mayor Vaughan in series two, having already appropriated his real name for the town, the affection was more evident. Brown was allowed to show his talent as a comic performer, rather than simply functioning as a quaint grotesque. Nevertheless, Reeves was clearly attracted to traditional TV formats like variety, the quiz show (*Shooting Stars* [BBC2, 1995–7, 2002]) and even *Generation Game*-like game shows featuring members of the public (*Families at War* [BBC1, 1999]).

Reeves and Mortimer were often compared with Morecambe and Wise (a comparison they did little to discourage), even though Eric and Ernie are often mobilised in nostalgic accounts of 'one nation' TV uniting audiences rather than dividing them into cult factions. Other unfashionable comic performers became credible names to cite as influences, such as the Two Ronnies and Dick Emery. Emery's influence on modern sketch comedy is particularly evident. His BBC1 series (1963–81) featured a gallery of regular characters with distinctive traits and catchphrases, of which the most enduring is 'You are awful, but I like you!' There was voluptuous maneater Mandy (see: *Little Britain's* Bubbles DeVere), spinsterish Hettie (surely the basis for Cathy Carter Smith, Pauline's nemesis), gay Clarence (see: Herr Lipp, *Little Britain's* Sebastian and Dafydd, Catherine Tate's 'How *very* dare you!' character), and phlegmy old man Lampwick (*The Fast Show's* Unlucky Alf *and* Coughing Bob Fleming). The catchphrase dominated new comedy, from 'You wouldn't let it lie!' to 'Am I bothered, though?', and the League would add several to the pantheon: 'This is a local shop for local people, there's nothing for you here'; 'Hello, hello, what's all this shouting? We'll have no trouble here!'; 'hokey cokey, pig in a pokey'; 'Hello Dave'.

The shift from the alternative to the post-alternative was in some ways also a socio-geographic one. While a number of alternative comedians had northern backgrounds, 80s' comedy manifested a metropolitan antipathy towards the 'north'. Provincial and bigoted, the north was equated with mother-in-law jokes, racism, homophobia and bingo. Roland Muldoon of Cartoon Archetypical Slogan Theatre (could they sound any more like Legz Akimbo?) distils this phobic reaction:

22

> Travelling in the North we began to realise that they're not necessarily into
> theatre – you would be playing in a trade union centre for example and you
> could see that there was going to be bingo another night; we could see that
> the real culture of the North was this bland kind of northern
> entertainment.[24]

While post-alternative comedy is diverse, it did encompass a new
regionalism in which the north was prominent. An important bridge
between the alternative comedy of the 1980s and the new comedy of the
1990s was the comic *Viz* (1979–). Like the alternative comedians, *Viz*
was confrontational and violent, but it was also aggressively regional
and rather less politically aligned. Full of north-east slang and
prodigiously filthy, it could be puerile and lairy as often as it was
cuttingly satirical. It struck a chord with Jeremy Dyson: 'you could sense
like-minded people, who were very sharp, and they kind of "got" the
country. And I think their view of Britain was not unlike the Royston
Vasey view of Britain.' 'Northern' comedy would take many forms from
the early 90s, but its presence was strongly felt. According to Jonathan
Ross, the 'northernness' of Reeves and Mortimer was part of their
appeal, with '(t)heir unapologetic use of phrases and terms that were
peculiar to their region, *or seemed like they might be to people from the
south* (my emphasis)'.[25] Like the League, Reeves and Mortimer were
northerners who lived in London, arguably producing a more
ambivalent regional identity than the more affectionate comedy of Peter
Kay or Caroline Aherne; grotesque and strange rather than nostalgic
and affirmative.

    Reeves and Mortimer displayed a silliness that set them apart
from the more confrontational comedy that preceded them ('I'm glad to
see the Red Arrows are still flying formation – makes my job a lot
easier.') But there is also a freakish dimension that links them to the
League. Reeves's impersonation of Loyd Grossman in *The Smell of
Reeves and Mortimer* equips him with a bulbous forehead, a knife and
fork extending from his forefingers as he floats on the air, accompanied
by church bells. *Bang Bang, It's Reeves and Mortimer* featured a

recurring sketch, 'The Club', a mockumentary about a grim nightclub in Hull, pitched somewhere between Vasey and *Peter Kay's Phoenix Nights* (Channel 4, 2001–2). 'The Club' would form the basis of *Catterick* (BBC3, 2005), Vic and Bob's apparent bid to join the 'dark comedy' club. According to Ben Thompson, Reeves initially saw the League as unwelcome rivals (just as the League sometimes seemed slightly resentful of *Little Britain*'s success),[26] but Dyson and Gatiss wrote an episode of the remake of *Randall and Hopkirk (Deceased)* (BBC1, 2000, 2001), and the Gents provided cameos in the series. Gatiss appeared briefly in *Catterick*, but Shearsmith stole the show as psychotic mother's boy Tony. While incandescent rage isn't exactly a stretch for Shearsmith, here was a character – flossing his teeth until they bled, torturing someone with a nostril-hair remover – who made Geoff Tipps seem positively sunny in comparison.

Dark Materials

'Blacker than Black Is Back' declares the DVD sleeve of *Nighty Night* series two, Julia Davis's near-the-knuckle sitcom about a sociopathic beautician who leaves a trail of corpses and torments the MS-afflicted wife of the object of her affections. The programme was identified as part of a trend that included *Human Remains* (BBC2, 2000), Chris Morris's *Jam* (Channel 4, 2000) and *Funland* (BBC3, 2005). 'Dark comedy' was a cultish comic subgenre in which the League were prime movers; Gatiss appeared in, and contributed material to, *Nighty Night*, while Dyson co-wrote *Funland*. The term implies a lineage from 'Black Comedy', the literary label applied to writers as diverse as Joseph Heller, Kurt Vonnegut, Harold Pinter and Joe Orton. *Radio Times* wondered whether comedy was the 'new drama', citing the League, *I'm Alan Partridge* (BBC2, 1997–2002), *The Office* and *Phoenix Nights* as shows which were 'frequently bleak and often despairing, filled with unsympathetic characters who ... are uncomfortably authentic in ways that TV dramas cannot seem to achieve'.[27] But as a *Zeitgeist* term, 'dark comedy' also recalls the way the word 'sick' circulated in the USA in the late 1950s, referring to disparate phenomena like Lenny Bruce, *Mad magazine* and 'dead baby' jokes.[28] 'Black' and 'Dark' imply a seriousness of purpose; as J. L Styan puts it, 'to counter the glibness of the fixed idea and to block a too easy response'.[29] 'Sick', on the other hand, suggests something more callous and puerile, even if 50s' 'sick' is sometimes taken as a cathartic response to the repressions and pieties of the period.[30]

I want to venture two suggestions about 'dark comedy' on British TV. First, it is perhaps best seen as a mixture of the 'Black' and the 'sick', sometimes vaguely satirical but rarely attributable to an especially noble agenda. Second, it is defined by its institutional and media context, by testing the boundaries of what is permissible on broadcast TV, particularly within a genre that is ostensibly a branch of 'light entertainment'. With that in mind, 'dark comedy' arguably begins with Monty Python's 'The Undertaker's Sketch', written by and starring Graham Chapman and John Cleese, and broadcast as the final sequence in their second series (BBC2, 1970). Chapman is the undertaker, Cleese the customer who arrives with his mother's corpse in a sack. Chapman talks him through the options (burial, cremation, dumping her in the Thames) before they decide on cooking and eating her. 'If you feel guilty afterwards, we can dig a grave and you can throw up in it', he explains. There are boos and catcalls from the audience, who finally rush the studio stage. That they rather overplay their collective part gives the game away before the National Anthem kicks in and everyone, Pythons and rioting audience alike, stands to attention. The inclusion of the protesting audience was the condition for the BBC sanctioning a sketch that had caused considerable concern; it frames it self-consciously as being 'unacceptable'.[31] No TV comedy sketch had gone so far into calculated tastelessness before, and Python would never go so far on TV again. One can read the sketch as an assault on the 'fixed idea' and 'easy response', or as evidence of an adolescent and heartless desire to shock and offend. In fact, it's probably a bit of both. Then again, if we step back into canonical 'black comedy', let's not forget that Joe Orton, whose

25

mischievous 'bad taste' has a lot in common with recent 'dark comedy', started out by defacing library books with obscenities.

Some of the League's 'darkness' is inextricable from their love of the Gothic, but some of their darkest material owes little to generic horror, like Mick McNamara, the Stumphole Cavern tour guide haunted by his responsibility for a boy's death in the caves. According to Henri Bergson, 'the comic demands something like a momentary anaesthesia of the heart', an evacuation of empathy and sentiment; 'look upon life as a disinterested spectator: many a drama will turn into a comedy'.[32] 'Stumphole Cavern' is justly celebrated as one of the League's classic sketches. It's effectively a monologue, and one that displays the influence of Alan Bennett's *Talking Heads* (BBC2, 1988, 1998) in its mixture of tragedy and comedy. The TV version (1.5) slightly over-literalises some of the gags, like the limestone formation named after Errol Flynn,[33] but Gatiss's performance more than carries the day. The humour initially derives from Mick's monotone delivery and his appearance (cagoule with shorts, shoes and socks) and Stumphole's underwhelming reputation as 'Royston Vasey's second finest showcase'. But even Stumphole's secondary status has a ghastly origin, comparative to rival Redscar's '100 per cent safety record'. With a singular lack of enthusiasm, Mick extols the virtues of the cave or regales his audience with its TV legacy – episodes of *Doctor Who*, *Bulman* (Granada/ITV, 1985–7), and, more ominously, 'Michael Buerk and the 999 team'. It becomes apparent, however, that Mick's voice signals not boredom but clinical depression, a condition brought about by a terrible incident; 'I myself am not fond of the darkness. I sleep with the light on now. It's in the darkness I see the boy's face – eyes protruding, tongue out, black.' As he demonstrates the stalactites' resemblance to various figures, the tour and his terrible need to speak of his guilt become conjoined:

> This one over here, people say to me, 'Mick, that doesn't look like anything at all', but I don't know. When I look at it, I seem to see a little pair of hands clutching at a slippery wet rope, sliding down, down into the dark water. Sometimes, I'll stand here for hours [pregnant pause] just looking at it.

Stumphole Cavern: 'a little pair of hands clutching at a slippery wet rope'

Tragedy and banality are united by a speech clearly delivered with numbing regularity in a subterranean purgatory. The sketch hinges precisely on that which ought not to be funny, but the comic dimension is clear. Mick's behaviour is inappropriate, depressing his paying audience with tales of drowned children, but filled with pathos. It's this pathos that keeps 'Stumphole Cavern' from being as contentious as some of the 'Dark Comedy' broadcast during this period.

27

Thirty years after Python's undertaker, Chris Morris's *Jam* gave a disturbing inflection to Bergson's notion of being anaesthetised. Its woozy visuals and soundscapes invited analogies with ambient music and bad drugs, but the material was unlikely to let you lapse into unconsciousness. The distraught parents of a missing child sing an impromptu, pleading song at a press conference, accompanying themselves on a xylophone. Someone presents a tiny coffin to a woman who has just had a termination. A doctor offers telephone sex to raise money for a child with head cancer – 'I'm coming so hard that spunk is shooting out of your eyes.'

Jam was broadcast shortly after the second series of the League, and it was not uncommon to see them compared. 'There are lines we wouldn't cross', Jeremy Dyson told one interviewer, 'and we're only worried about whether something makes us laugh.'[34] Nevertheless, series two would produce one of the League's most controversial sketches (2.4). It features Vinnie and Reenie, two elderly charity-shop workers. Although more detailed and convincingly made up, they are the closest the League get to the Pythons' 'Pepperpots', working-class women with shrill voices. Through a combination of poor hearing and attention spans that quickly lose the thread of a conversation, they transform the simplest transactions into endless sagas or pretexts for making tea. Donations and purchases get confused and phrases are repeated like a kind of echolalia ('It's a cassette'/'It's a cassette, is it?') When corrected, they quickly take offence – 'No need to be rude, dear!' – but are peculiarly acquisitive about plastic bags. Mrs Beasley, a minor character who will resurface briefly in series three, arrives with a bag of baby's clothes and a teddy bear. The familiar schtick kicks in – 'It's a teddy, is it?' – but there is a more pressing concern.

28

> REENIE: We can't take it without a special mark.
> MRS BEASLEY: Why not?
> VINNIE: It's not safe, dear. All the safe ones have got a special mark. It could have glass in it, this.
> REENIE: Or sand, dear.
> VINNIE: Give this to a kiddie, dear, it could die.
> REENIE: It's a death trap, it wouldn't be right if we took it.
> (Mrs Beasley is too upset to speak)
> VINNIE: I think The Spastics will have it, though, dear.
> REENIE: Yeah, they'll take anything!

They give her the teddy back, and turn to their other obsession, keeping the plastic bag, but that triggers a further investigation into special marks. Does the bag have one? 'You could kill a kiddie with this', insists Reenie as Mrs Beasley sinks to the floor in tears. We have long since worked out why the clothes (unceremoniously dropped on the floor as they scrutinise the bag) and the teddy are no longer needed. The sketch

Reenie and Vinnie: 'Has it got a special mark?'

Reenie and Mrs Beasley: 'You could kill a kiddie with this!'

had played to no conspicuous offence in the radio series, where the dead child was even named as 'little Karen', but the television version had a more mixed reception. The *Independent*'s Brian Viner was among those unamused:

> I don't object to the theory that you can extract humour from anything if you squeeze hard enough, and I'm all for comedy as a kind of shock therapy, but everyone has their limits and this breached mine. Maybe I'm getting old. At any rate I'm old enough to have friends whose children have died.[35]

It would be unconscionably glib to trivialise the latter comment (even if one senses a touch of moral blackmail), and yet two issues need to be raised here. The first is that jokes land indiscriminately, unaware of who might be in their vicinity and vulnerable to their impact. It has long been accepted that death is a valid, and even necessary, subject for comedy, even as most people are aware that there will be times in their lives when they are unlikely to appreciate the joke. Second, then, is infant mortality more sacrosanct than other kinds of bereavement? Moreover, can *any* subject be regarded as unsuitable for comedy? I would suggest that the answer has to be no, given the social and psychological function of humour (although that's easy enough to say in the abstract). The question is whether some treatments are more palatable than others.

If the League touched on infant mortality, *Jam* seemed to positively pounce on it, with its foetus-coffins (disturbingly reminiscent of the Dentons' toad-coffins) and a sketch that led the Broadcast Complaints Commission to judge the programme 'unacceptable'. A plumber arrives at a woman's house, assuming that he's been called to fix the boiler, but learns differently: 'did I say boiler? Sorry, I meant baby'. A plumber, she reasons, is good at fixing things, and her three-week-old baby has 'stopped working'. 'It's just tubes really, isn't it, and I'm sure you'd have a go.' Initially apprehensive, at £1,000 an hour, he's prepared to try. He plumbs the baby into the central heating. There's even a tap that makes him gurgle and sends steam from his mouth, and the mother coos appreciatively.

The two sketches deal with the same taboo quite differently. The *Jam* sketch is more disturbing, and there's a sense that it's quite prepared not to be found funny. The music is ominous, but then develops an incongruous trip-hop beat. The steam emerging from the baby's mouth is a detail that most horror films wouldn't go near. The central idea, the assumption that babies and boilers can be fixed in the same way, is absurd (particularly when proved correct), but it isn't necessarily funny. If the audience isn't exactly offended, it may be left uncertain of how to react. The League, on the other hand, signal the comic to us more clearly. The charity-shop sketch is a riff on inappropriate behaviour and crossed signals. Unlike *Jam*, the League were still using recorded laughter in series two. The audience laughter reassures us that we aren't bad people for laughing, but confirms in its tone that it's a *risky* kind of laughter. If we are regular viewers, we have met Vinnie and Reenie earlier in series two and know their routine, the obsession with bags, the tea-making, the vehemence towards their rivals 'The Spastics' and offscreen co-worker 'that Merrill'. How might the sketch feel if Mrs Beasley wasn't played by Mark Gatiss, but by an actress? Does the cross-dressing trivialise something tragic or render it easier to take as comedy by underlining the artifice of the sketch format? Mrs Beasley is less grotesque than Vinnie and Reenie, but less convincingly 'feminine' than some of the other cross-dressing parts (she's a little like Val Denton in a different wig). But if this keeps her in the realm of the comic, offers some protection against the horrible tragedy, Gatiss plays it straight enough for her grief to be oddly affecting.

31

Sometimes the League err on the side of caution. Mr Foot, a series one character, has problems talking to disabled people; the more he tries to display an enlightened attitude, the more his prejudices break through. A sketch with a young man in a wheelchair (1.5) originally concluded with Mr Foot's repressed anxieties finally exploding – 'fucking cripple!'. The broadcast version concludes with his catchphrase, 'Was it something I said?'. In other material, they seem to have shocked even themselves. Herr Lipp's sojourn in Royston Vasey

Herr Lipp says goodbye to Justin

ends with his failed date-rape of schoolboy Justin. He leaves him buried alive in the front garden, with a tube for oxygen (a tiny moving ball confirms Justin's horrible existence) (2.6). 'This is the most disgusting thing we've ever committed to screen', Dyson suggests on the DVD commentary, while Gatiss observes the studio audience's quietly shocked reaction. Such material might explain why the second series started to lose viewers. For some, it was dark at the expense of being funny. And yet, as Geoff King argues, comedy can be used 'dangerously' in otherwise dark and non-comic material, challenging the audience to walk a 'dangerous' line on 'the outer limits of the darkest comedy'.[36] For the cult viewer, the challenge is to find the comic within such disturbing material.

The League were only officially censured once. There had been complaints to the Broadcast Standards Commission about Legz Akimbo Theatre Company's slogan 'Put Yourself into a Child', others about Mr Foot patronising the disabled, another that Herr Lipp 'trivialised' paedophilia, but each was rejected. However, objections to Bernice's use of the word 'mongs' in the Christmas Special were upheld,[37] even though the Reverend is even more clearly signalled as a bigoted character than well-meaning Mr Foot, memorably describing Legz Akimbo as 'AIDS in a van'. The League's response is telling, a justifiable feeling of over-reaction mixed with juvenile defiance. In *The Making of Series Three* (BBC Choice, 2002), they respond to the complaint. 'In our defence, we have a letter from a disabled person ...' begins Gatiss. 'From a mong?' interjects Dyson, not entirely helpfully, before Gatiss recovers and continues: '... saying that the word "mong" is being reclaimed, like "nigger" and "queer" and that it is used by several people and they were very glad we'd used it, so I'm going to take *that* to the ITC'. But, Pemberton objects, 'that makes out like we're politically correct'. Given the way that they have continued to defiantly use the word (in *The League of Gentlemen's Apocalypse*, for example), the latter accusation possibly troubles them more.

Furnished Worlds and Thick Texts

During an interview with Gatiss and Pemberton on *The Johnny Vaughan Show* (BBC Choice, 2002), Vaughan suggests that the series' fans are 'one down from your sci-fi fans'. Gatiss agrees that there is a similarity to the kind of obsessive fandom associated with fantasy and science fiction: 'It's a kind of enclosed world, like *Star Trek*, and I think that's what people respond to. They like to know where bits of the town are.' In a famous, if now unfashionable, essay on cult cinema, Umberto Eco identifies one of the preconditions of cultdom.

33

> It must provide a completely furnished world so that its fans can quote characters and episodes as if they were aspects of the fan's sectarian world, a world about which one can make up quizzes and play trivia games so that adepts of the sect recognise each other through a shared expertise.[38]

Take Eco out of context (he's writing about *Casablanca* [1943]) and one might think he has *Buffy the Vampire Slayer* (WB, 1997–2001, UPN, 2002–3) or *Lost* (ABC, 2004–) in mind. If the idea now seems better suited to television than film, it is perhaps more surprising to find a relevance to TV comedy, which we might associate with small rather than expansive worlds. It is not, of course, uncommon for comedy fans to quote heavily; if we are familiar with the negative stereotype of the sci-fi 'anorak', we probably also know of the comedy obsessive (parodied through *The Fast Show*'s Colin Hunt) forever reeling off sketches and catchphrases. What is distinctive about *The League* and a few other recent comedies (*Spaced*, *The Mighty Boosh*) is the notion of a 'world' that one can immerse oneself in. *The Mighty Boosh* had its 'Zooniverse' in series one, while series two was distinctively furnished by visual designer Tim Hope, drawing on stylised back-projection, animation and model work that gave a unique realisation to a world inflected by pop subcultures and occupied by Shoreditch shamen, talking moons, demonic nanas and a transsexual fish-man with a 'mangina' and a weakness for Bailey's Irish Cream. Royston Vasey was a completely furnished world even before it was Vasey. The pitch for *On the Town with the League of Gentlemen* describes Spent (as it was then) as 'bigger than a village but smaller than a city ... about the size of Wakefield' and having 'far too many pubs'.[39] The pitch provides a wealth of detail, from the town's estates – upmarket Swanmills, rough Redhawk 'plagued by wasps every summer' – to buildings like Oriel House (the Jobcentre), the pub Swiss Cottage ('the Swiss'), Indian (Shebabs) and Italian (Luigi's) restaurants, or shops like Hackett and Baines 'where you get your school uniform'.[40] Little of this detail could be incorporated explicitly into the radio show, more would be realised on television. Some maintained an offscreen existence.

The 'furnishing' of Vasey would happen in two ways. First, Grenville Horner would bring a high level of design intensity to the characters' environments. The Dentons' home is defined by what Dyson calls 'particularly upsetting wallpaper', protective coverings and a multitude of toad ornaments. For Les McQueen, the design team created a record collection that would remain largely invisible; 'every single record was absolutely correct', claims Dyson.[41] When Les

The Dentons: upsetting wallpaper, plastic coverings and coordinated toads

35

Les McQueen's record collection and signed album covers

removes Creme Brulee's 'Just Desserts' from pride of place in the pile
(1.2), we might just glimpse a Bucks Fizz LP behind it, but we can clearly
see album covers by Smokie (signed!) and Pilot on the wall. With its 70s'
stylings, I find myself most drawn to Les's flat, but not necessarily his
vinyl collection.

Second, Vasey would be mapped indelibly onto Hadfield in Derbyshire, seeming to blur the line between the fictional town and the real location. Hadfield/Vasey became the object of what Matt Hills calls 'cult geography', where a 'sacred place' is used to 'anchor and legitimate cult fans' attachments'.[42] Fans staged meet-ups or made individual pilgrimages to see the war memorial, buy 'Special Stuff' from Mettricks the butchers or stroll through 'bummer's alley' on the way to the pub.[43] 'Cult geography' is connected to 'location tourism',[44] which in the UK has transformed towns in the East Midlands and Yorkshire into '*Peak Practice* country' or '*Last of the Summer Wine* country'. It is perhaps the province of the cultist to want to visit '*League of Gentlemen* country'. *Hadfield, The Real Royston Vasey* (LocalVideos.co.uk, 2002) offers a strange convergence of organised fandom and the Derbyshire Heritage Centre. The DVD seems to be largely designed to reinvigorate Hadfield tourism in the same way that *Last of the Summer Wine* (BBC1, 1973–) did for Holmforth. Instead, as we are taken on a tour of the series' locations, some of them derelict, it inadvertently creates the impression that the town only comes to life when the series is being filmed or its fans visit. If this seems to authenticate Hadfield's 'Vaseyness', it also makes for an unprepossessing travelogue to which only a fan expecting a town as grim as that in the series might respond. The DVD only picks up when fans converge in full costume on the Mason's Arms, the pub frequented by Geoff, Mike and Brian.

The League of Gentlemen is very much a TV comedy of the DVD age, a medium that helps cement classic status, snatching the potentially ephemeral from the broadcast flow and enshrining it in box sets, enriching it with commentaries, outtakes, extra features and 'Easter eggs'. It also provides another key to the immersiveness of the series. Roz Kaveney has coined the phrase 'thick text' to characterise the way media like DVD has redefined textuality; 'we accept that all texts are not only a product of the creative process but contain all the stages of that process within them like scars or vestigial organs'.[45] I want here to take the DVD commentary as one of these 'vestigial organs', one that ostensibly reflects on the text, but may in fact become part of it. It may even take on a greater importance for some fans. One poster on lofg.com reflects a not uncommon view of the League's commentaries; 'I only ever watch the series with the commentary on'. If there is an 'official' view of the DVD commentary, it is that it offers a canonical insight into the film or programme, ideally from a director or writer. Certainly the League's commentaries are informative with regard to the creative process, from writing to production. But commentaries may offer other pleasures. In the case of a comedy DVD, for example, we might expect the commentary to be comic in its own right. According to Pemberton:

> I was talking to someone about the DVDs the other day, and he was referring to the commentaries more than the content of the programme ... You realize that you sit there and blabber on for three hours, and people actually listen to it – they get enjoyment from it. He was quoting bits of the commentary back to me.[46]

It's a measure of the reputation the League have that in 2005 they performed a live commentary for their feature film at London's Prince Charles cinema.

In addition to offering a subsidiary, spontaneous but eminently quotable comic performance, one of the key pleasures offered is an effect, however illusory, of intimacy. As the lofg.com fan quoted above puts it, 'When you listen to them it's like listening to a great private conversation between best friends.' The commentaries have a narrative integrity of their own, operating as a kind of shadow text to the series. By series three, they're as entertaining as ever, but there is an undertone of discontent. 'It's like therapy, isn't it?' comments Dyson early on. Distinct personae emerge. Pemberton is always funny, but slightly more circumspect than the others. Shearsmith can be entertainingly curmudgeonly, never more so than on the series three commentary, where he constantly seems on the point of turning into Geoff Tipps: 'So, end of second episode and hopefully it becomes apparent to people *how clever we're being* ... . Not just sketches any more, oh no ... . Right, see

37

you for episode 3, if you can be bothered!' Gatiss can be outrageous and forthright, whether settling accounts with an extra ('fucking idiot') or musing on Jamie Bell's 'tight little body', while one has to be impressed by Dyson's capacity (in this company) for eliciting shocked responses of '*Jeremy!*' One could quote all day. Here's Gatiss's summation of Pop: 'sentimentality mixed with brute violence. It's like crying at a christening and then punching the baby in the face.' Dyson gives us an entirely new way of seeing the sequence where Hilary Briss meets Maurice in a public toilet. 'I love Hilary sizing him up ... and he reaches a conclusion and dismisses him ... . He's seen into his soul through his cock.' There are catchphrases and running jokes ('Oh, it's a shame for him', 'Homoerotic opening scene'). There is even an equivalent to the Special Stuff, an enigma to which only they know the answer. Who are the dummy in the charity shop and drab Judith meant to resemble?[47] Above all, there is the pleasure of amusing people making each other laugh, with periodic cries of 'You can't say that!' reinforcing the impression of unmediated access (even if there are occasional silences to cover possibly libellous exchanges).

38

    The commentary expands the 'world' that the cult fan feels able to inhabit, from the fictional Vasey to the 'real' Gents. Little wonder then that they felt able to play on this slippage in their feature film where these two worlds interact. *The League of Gentlemen's Apocalypse* is very much about the series' status as a 'thick text', one that overflows, if not into the real world then into other fictional worlds, where the inhabitants of Vasey interact with fictionalised versions of the Gents themselves and characters from another (Gothic, historical) story. In contradiction of Eco, Sara Gwenllian Jones argues that cult TV fascinates its fans by offering '*incompletely* furnished worlds' that constitute an 'invitation to imagine' an extended world beyond the televised text.[48] Vasey may be a small town, but it's a big 'world'.

3 Local

Prior to *The League of Gentlemen*'s first broadcast on Monday 11 January 1999, *Radio Times* promised 'characters who would not look out of place in *Twin Peaks* or *The Fast Show*'.[49] Many such comparisons circulated, but this was the most succinct: instantly recognisable characters with catchphrases that would imprint themselves on popular culture, and a strange town with dark secrets. *The Fast Show* had been the most celebrated British sketch show in recent years and, while it was known for its speed and repetitive catchphrases, it also produced characters with the capacity for development and comic pathos. Among their best loved were Ralph (Charlie Higson) and Ted (Paul Whitehouse), a country Lord and the Irish groundsman he is palpably in love with; it came as little surprise that they would spin off into a one-off special of their own. Sketches have their modern origins in music hall, vaudeville and burlesque, distinguished from other kinds of variety show comic performance by the presence of characters, fictional settings, dialogue and causal events.[50] This doesn't preclude an element of seriality, however, something the League had already approached in their Canal Café shows and even more suited to a radio or TV series. 'By definition a sketch is a quick sort of thumbnail thing', says Gatiss, 'but within that if you have the skills to do it then you can suggest an awful lot of backstory, history and pain.'

On the Town with the League of Gentlemen (Radio 4, 1997) constitutes a midway point to the format of the TV series. It confined itself to those characters that could be plausibly incorporated into the town that would bind the series into something resembling a continuing narrative. At this stage, this excluded Tubbs and Edward, such a defining feature of the TV series. Bernice became a DJ and agony aunt on Spent FM, but would find her most satisfying incarnation on TV as Royston Vasey's vicar, delivering ferocious sermons to tearful primary schoolchildren or berating the arrogance of the disabled from the pulpit. Some of the material developed specially for the radio show uses the sensory 'incompleteness' of the medium; Mr Ingleby the world's smallest shopkeeper ('lift me up'),[51] or a sequence where we discover that Harvey Denton has joined Benjamin in the bath during one of his lectures. Barbara, the transsexual cab driver, is ostensibly a radio character, too,[52] the humour resting on her bodily secrets being revealed verbally and the contrast between Pemberton's gruff voice and the unremitting gynaecological detail: nipples like bullets, bed 'like a butcher's slab'. This would translate to TV through a visual reticence about Barbara, a fragmented presence revealed only through glimpses of hairy chest and legs, high-heeled shoes squeezed onto manly feet, Pemberton's voice dubbed over another actor whom we never fully saw. Barbara has more of a storyline on radio, though, including meeting Mr Ingleby through the Close Encounters dating agency and finally achieving full, glamorous womanhood (voiced by Sally Phillips). *On the Town* featured a number of celebrated stage sketches, including 'Mau Mau', 'Egregious' (in which Ross turns the tables on Pauline during a role-play session), 'Stumphole Cavern' and Legz Akimbo's 'Everybody Out', 'a show about homosexuality aimed at 9–12 year olds'. With Tubbs and Edward on hiatus, the Dentons are very much the narrative centre of *On the Town*, with a growing emphasis on Benjamin's efforts to escape. He arrives for an interview at the local plant (a plastics factory in the TV series), and is soon threatened by his uncle's Dr Moreau-like scheme to turn him into a Toad–Human hybrid. Close behind is social security restart officer Pauline and her 'dole scum', slack-jawed 'Mickey-luv' and educated, antagonistic Ross. As in the final episode of series one on TV, Ross later declares that he has been conducting an internal investigation of Pauline, but the radio series reveals this as a prank that backfires, and

Pauline emerges more triumphant than she will be in her small-screen incarnation. Moreover, Ross ends up as a pathetic figure rather than righteous nemesis, slightly contradicting the League's claims that he only progressed to villainy in response to the TV audience's hostility to the character.

The TV series would ditch some of the characters from the radio show, including Gatiss's PE teacher Mr McCunn, who turns every class into a competitive battle, even when covering RE ('Two teams. Pharaohs. Israelites. Clear a space, come out fighting.') In turn, others would be added, not only the Tattsyrups and their Local Shop, but more recent characters developed in the shows at Highgate. Les McQueen joined Chinnery and Alvin in what we might call a trio of 'Michael Palin' characters played by Gatiss and co-written with Dyson. 'I don't actually like bright, sharp, clever, pushy people', the former Python has said, 'so I tend to go for the sort of characters that would infuriate them.'[53] Palin archetypes include Mr Pither in Python's 'Cycling Tour' episode (1972) and the eponymous hero of 'The Testing of Eric Olthwaite' in *Ripping Yarns* (BBC2, 1977). Like Eric's obsession with rainfall figures and shovels, Les and Alvin are good-natured bores, similarly oblivious to the tedium they inflict. They exist in a crueller world than Palin's, though, and emerge rather less victorious. Les's story comes to a sad end, swindled out of his redundancy money by Creme Brulee, who have reformed without him. As this terrible realisation dawns, his glam-rock collar wilts in sympathy (2.5). At the other extreme, Pop, created by Dyson for Pemberton, is one of the League's most terrifying characters. Ethnically ambiguous (Greek? Italian? Russian?), he is a virtual satyr, bestial and mercurial, sentimental about his sons as he rewards them with gruesome-looking porn. The two sides of Pop are captured by his favourite videos, *Watership Down* (he croons 'Bright Eyes' to his tearful son Al after frightening off his girlfriend) and *The Assmaster*. He manifests both the threat, and unpredictable outbursts, of violence, and is a genuinely disturbing sexual predator, over-intimate with Al's girlfriend Trish (a discomfort played straight), or watching his tenants in intimate situations on close-circuit TV. If the

41

League offer some unflattering depictions of older women, Pop is their fullest manifestation of monstrous masculinity, a bad father of frightening proportions. He rules a family evacuated of women, drenched in porn and fearful of effeminacy ('Mary-Queens'), and committed to making men of his terrified sons, including adoptive 'sons' like tenant Gary. He's the sort of hairy patriarch Robert Bly seems to long for (and probably deserves) in his Man-ifesto *Iron John*, but these boys long to escape his bullying tyranny. Richie is ejected from the family when some boys steal chocolate bars from the family newsstand he is left in charge of. The broadcast version omits the pay-off – I'm not sure 'punchline' is the word – that Richie has orchestrated his own downfall and ejection from the family ('fuck you, Pop'), stealing the Maverick bars himself (1.2). Described in these terms, this isn't sounding much like a comedy, and Pop is one of those figures who walk a fine line between comedy and something murkier. Some of the comedy lies in his grossness, settling down for a pot noodle and a wank as he spies on his tenants, or serving hideous food to Trish and Al. Then there are his flamboyant gestures, such as his strange face-slapping manoeuvre[54] or flapping his hands beneath his chin to signify homosexuality. His self-deluding sentimentality is comic, as is the absurdity of a newsagent who views himself as the architect of some great empire, the immigrant making it big as Godfather of confectionary. The immigrant adjusting to a new home is a comedy archetype, like Harry Enfield's Stavros, but rarely this extreme.

For a sketch review-turned radio show, *The League of Gentlemen* arrived fully formed as a televisual experience. The 'fourth wall' shooting of some sequences (the Dentons, the Local Shop) gives them a sitcom quality, but other scenes adopt a more 'cinematic' visual style. There is the signature craning-up to the war memorial in the title sequences, or the overhead shot that captures Herr Lipp's rapture on first seeing schoolboy Justin (2.1). This 'cinematic' styling often works through intertextual pastiche. As Al and Richie wait for their father at a warehouse, the low-angled camera circles them *Reservoir Dogs*-style before Pop materialises in a shaft of light through a window (1.2). Other

'Michael Palin' character: Les and wilting collar

Monstrous father: Pop terrorises his sons

Predatory satyr: Pop and Trish

sequences trade on gothic conventions, like the nocturnal drive through the woods that pastiches *Night of the Demon* (1957) in the opening scene of 2.4 as Hilary collects a 'special delivery'. The series is packed with visual jokes, most densely organised in the 'quickies' that populate the title sequences. Take 2.1's opening titles, for example: another variant on the *Full Monty* poster gags, *The Shull Monty* (one of several Jewish jokes Dyson injected into the series); Pop leaves the off-licence (a revolving sign spells out 'Cheap/Booze') for the Sensations Massage Parlour (another reads 'Blow/Jobs'); Vinnie drives her mobility vehicle at a snail's pace in front of a fire engine; a handle breaks off a portaloo, depositing its occupant on the pavement in a torrent of water; a flyer reads 'Earn £££££'s Contract Killing. No experience necessary'. Equally important was the elaborate appearance of the characters formerly performed in tux-and-tie, 'fixed' for good through an array of bodysuits and make-up designs. The more freakish characters attracted

'Fourth wall' shooting style:
Martin enters the Local Shop

Signature crane shot:
the war memorial

Movie pastiche: Pop materialises in
the *Reservoir Dogs* scene

Opening title 'quickies' ...
The Shull Monty

Revolving sign at Sensations Massage Parlour

The Dentons' 'Nude Day'　　　　Comic physiognomies:
　　　　　　　　　　　　　　　　Cathy Carter Smith

most attention, as did the naked bodysuits worn by Tubbs, in a bizarre
parody of Britt Ekland's *Wicker Man* dance, and the Dentons during
'Nude Day'. Comic physiognomies run through the series. Cathy Carter
Smith's face appears to have sustained long-term damage from
prolonged gurning, topped off by crimson batwings for a mouth; her
expression as Mickey stands on his chair in support of Pauline is
grotesquely eloquent (2.1). More subtle effects hinge on an array of
unhealthy skin tones and unflattering hair; Geoff's 'burnt' features and
thinning curls, Hilary's ruddy cheeks and mutton chops underlining the
depths of his depravity.

　　　As on radio, Benjamin is an important unifying feature of the
narrative in series one and two. At the end of series one, he encounters
Tubbs for the first time, following her to the Local Shop. As series two
begins, he escapes, mud-spattered and sparsely clad, and returns to the
Dentons clutching a 'precious thing' and croaking the word 'Local'
(think: 'Rosebud'). At the end of series two, he escapes the Dentons'
machinations and finds the 'precious thing' in his pocket, triggering a

45

flashback montage that will prompt him to lead an angry mob to the Local Shop (2.6). The arrival of the New Road is the notional storyline for series one, but it impacts most directly on Tubbs and Edward, threatening strangers and bringing their estranged son David back to them. Other characters mention the New Road, such as Hilary, the businessmen, and Bernice in one of her sermons, while Chinnery is affected more directly when called to examine the pig/monkey/sheep hybrid fashioned by Edward to frighten off the road-diggers. The 'Special Stuff' served by butcher Hilary Briss functions as a self-contained storyline in series one (apart from being served at Mike's wedding), but its enigmatic nature provides a cultish hook for series two. Analogous to pornography (sold under the counter to male clientele), hard drugs (dangerous when 'cut') and bestiality (Hilary's literally bovine wife), often assumed by viewers to be human meat,[55] it is linked to the nosebleed epidemic either directly or through its dilution. Written specifically for television, Hilary's scenes with his customers Maurice and Sam contain few obvious jokes, resting more on slow-burning innuendo, a veritable opera of 'significant' looks and pregnant pauses that forms a bridge to the less gag-based comedy of series three.

46

The nosebleed epidemic plays a bit more like a story arc than the New Road did, even though it really only directly affects subsidiary characters like Mayor Vaughan, Maurice and Sam. For our Vasey headliners, the epidemic is largely background noise as, for example, when we see Stella shout at some looters as a preface to another acrimonious bout with Charlie. But the enigma of the Special Stuff is a strong, teasing thread, and several episodes open or close with scenes dealing with the epidemic, like 2.5's grim fade-out on Sam and Maurice in Hilary's basement, blood trickling from their noses. In the final episode, it brings several storylines to a point of closure. Hilary narrowly avoids arrest, Mayor Vaughan dies, and Tubbs and Edward are blamed for the epidemic. There is a growing sense of narrative structure in the series, something that will become even more important in subsequent work.

Citizen Denton: Benjamin returns with a 'precious thing'

Benjamin finds the snow globe at the end of series two

Slow-burning innuendo: Sam, Hilary and the Special Stuff

Our Fiends in the North

For years, writers have sat on their fat arses, getting rich writing *lies* about real northern people! I want to do that, too.

Ollie Plimsolls, Legz Akimbo Theatre Company

We'd like to apologise to viewers in the north. It must be terrible for you.

TV announcer, *Victoria Wood: As Seen on TV* (BBC2 ,1985–6)

In interviews, the League have sometimes downplayed the regionality of their work, understandably wary, like Alan Bennett before them,[56] of journalistic clichés about the 'northern' sense of humour. When we categorise the four Gents as 'northern', we conflate Yorkshire (Dyson, Shearsmith), Lancashire (Pemberton) and County Durham (Gatiss), while Hadfield (if not Vasey) is in Derbyshire, technically in the East Midlands. The 'north' operates as one half of a cultural opposition, the mythology of the north–south divide in England emerging in nineteenth-century literature in response to industrialisation, with the north becoming the 'Land of the Working Classes'.[57] The 'north' is less a coherent space (where does it begin and end?) than a set of images and values that distinguish it from the metropolitan south; working class, industrial, hard, bleak (Orwell's 'strange country'), or, in more romantic representations, authentic, warm-hearted and industrious in contrast with the effete, pretentious south. As a 'northern' English town, Royston Vasey works at three levels. First, it plays to a non-northern perception of the north as grim, provincial (local), inhospitable to strangers, a cultural desert. Second, the series provides an antidote to sentimental views of the north (including those the north has of itself): warm-hearted and down-to-earth. Third, it offers to an 'insider' not a totalising image of the 'north', but the recognisability of a certain type of town. The series' popularity rests partly on the perception that there is a kind of 'truth' behind the caricature. As post-industrial town, Vasey represents modernity stopped in its tracks, abandoned like a rotting tooth. Many fans of the series know or remember their own 'Vasey';

mine is Cleckheaton in West Yorkshire, where I spent my early childhood, an industrial town whose industries had died. But while the series is authenticated by the League members' experience of such towns, they seem to have lived *near*, rather than *in*, them. As Dyson explains in a radio interview with Paul Jackson: 'Where we lived in Leeds, it was on the edge of the town. There were all those small towns around like Otley and Ilkley, and you grew up to be very wary of them because they *were* dangerous places'.[58]

The opening scenes of 'Welcome to Royston Vasey' (1.1) establish the town as liminal – 'neither nowt nor summat', as its inhabitants might say – on the boundary between town and countryside. Two city boys, Benjamin and his friend Martin, arrive separately on a would-be holiday. While Benjamin arrives by train, Martin arrives at the Local Shop by foot, on the margins of an already marginal town. One gets the impression that no one in Vasey has ever noticed the Local Shop until Benjamin leads angry torch-wielding villagers there at the end of series two. As Martin surveys the landscape, he sees the town's sinister tourist slogan, 'Welcome to Royston Vasey. You'll Never Leave!' The camera, representing his point of view, tilts up from the sign to an overview of the townscape. As Simon Morgan-Russell observes, the shot is strikingly reminiscent of what British film historians call 'That Long Shot of Our Town from That Hill'.[59] The phrase was first used in 1963 with reference to the 'Kitchen Sink' films, mostly set in northern industrial towns; 'That Long Shot' would also materialise in the opening titles of *Coronation Street* (ITV/Granada, 1960–). Andrew Higson characterises 'That Long Shot' in 1960s' Kitchen Sink as 'the voyeurism of one class looking at another',[60] middle-class audiences (and film directors) getting a tourist's eye view of the working classes. Rob Shields discerns a different kind of tourism, a 'gaze from that privileged position in which the South has been placed with respect to the North'.[61] Vasey certainly lends itself to a 'south centred gaze', but its potential meanings don't end there. In another discussion of 'That Long Shot', Terry Lovell speculates that a certain kind of 1960s' viewer might have viewed the Kitchen Sink movies as both 'insider' and 'outsider'. For the educated

49

(formerly) working-class male, the 'scholarship boy' who emerged in the early 20th century, 'That Long Shot' might embody 'not an outsider's perspective, but that of someone deeply implicated in and familiar with what is observed'.[62] It might therefore represent the point of view of someone looking back nostalgically at the kind of town in which they used to live. Clearly, nostalgia is not the word for the League's depiction of Royston Vasey, but it still draws on a degree of familiarity and 'insider' knowledge. In the 1960s, the 'full rich life' that scholarship boy Richard Hoggart celebrates in *The Uses of Literacy* (1957) was fading as the industrial towns were already in decline; for a contemporary audience, it persists largely as a set of generic images (and clichés), even though sitcoms like *Phoenix Nights* and *Early Doors* (BBC2, 2003–4) encompass images of northern warmth and community. In *The League of Gentlemen*'s version of 'That Long Shot', one might discern the viewpoint of someone who has left the north and regards it from the perspective of both 'northerner' and adopted 'southerner'. Like Alan Bennett (a Yorkshireman educated at Oxford), the League comprises liminal northerners, occupying a position somewhere between 'inside' and 'outside'.[63] Moreover, their use of 'That Long Shot' embodies a class difference, a gaze at a town that was not 'home', but the grim or dangerous town nearby. This viewpoint is embodied in the figure of Benjamin, a student through whose eyes we will experience much of the town and who binds the first two series together.

The name 'Royston Vasey' invites consideration of another kind of 'northernness'. Roy 'Chubby' Brown's first appearance as Mayor Vaughan finds him wrestling with his propensity for expletives (2.4). Interviewed live on *Look North* about the nosebleed epidemic, he's the essence of decorum until thanked at the end. 'It's a fucking pleasure', he replies, face falling beautifully at his inability to conceal his baser self. The scene also works as an in-joke about Brown's foul-mouthed persona. He rarely appears on British television and the gag finds him on his best behaviour for the BBC before reverting to form. 'Northern' humour is as phantasmatic as the 'north' itself; what exactly unites Brown, Les Dawson, Alan Bennett, Victoria Wood, Caroline

Martin looks up from the sign ...

... to *That* Long Shot

'It's a fucking pleasure': Roy 'Chubby Brown' as Mayor Vaughan

Aherne and Vic Reeves? Nevertheless, Jeremy Dyson has suggested that
there is 'something about the north, when presented authentically that
(is) intrinsically funny', while 'there is something about the north when
it is presented as a cliché that is excruciating'.[64] In other words, it is less
a question of there being such a thing as 'northern humour' than of it
being presented authentically. In social geographies of British comedy,
the north is the home of 'laffs'; working-men's clubs, pier-ends and,
above all, Blackpool, where 'Chubby' still plays to the weekend
stag-and-hen crowd. For Jeff Nuttall and Rodick Carmichael, the north
is synonymous with 'Us' humour, the comedy of survival and the
'perpetual celebration of common factors'.[65] 'Me' humour, implicitly
smug and southern, is defined by wit, wherein the comic is 'always in
some way demonstrating his superiority'.[66]

This distinction is harder to maintain now. There's little point
in pretending that the League are anything other than university-
educated, middle-class boys who established themselves in fringe
festivals rather than in brutal clubland. But they are not unique in
combining the 'clever' and the 'common'. Python were as fond of the
vulgar as they were of the intellectual, although they were sufficiently

erudite to be able to cite Rabelais or Bergson. Nevertheless, while 'Chubby' Brown claims to have found the League mystifying as often as they were hilarious, he doesn't exactly look out of place in the programme. In some ways, Nuttall and Carmichael romanticise the humour of the north, from Frank Randle, 'a visibly overflowing sewerage system',[68] to Les Dawson's 'subtle portrayal of the great Northern skepticism'.[69] But they also capture the moment when club comedy hardens, 'defensive against the Southerners and liberals and educators and soft-spoken immigrants'.[70] They memorably describe a nameless comic who appeared on Granada TV's club stand-up compendium *The Comedians* (1971–92), telling 'sour, even vicious' jokes, 'spat out from a face drawn into the staring, taut, near-bilious expression a drunken man possesses just before he completely loses his temper'.[71] This was everything the alternative comics of the 1980s saw as venal about 'northern' entertainment, but it isn't hard to picture him as a Reece Shearsmith character. In fact, he sounds exactly how Geoff might sound if he channelled his rage into his stand-up act. *The Comedians* partly inspired Trevor Griffiths's play *Comedians* (1975), where Geoff would fit quite well as he wrestles with the enigma of comedy. Since the death of Bernard Manning, 'Chubby' Brown is northern club comedy's surviving titan. Peter Kay represents a kinder version of this tradition, the funny bones know-how without the bigotry ('I'm not homophobic ... I'm not frightened of my house'). *Phoenix Nights* has some dark elements, but it is also a loving celebration of 'laffs' and a dying cultural tradition.

53

The *League of Gentlemen* is also considered a northern comedy series because it *sounds* northern, even to viewers who can't discern more specific regional variations within that broad categorisation. Dialect humour once played a key role in sustaining the north–south divide, allowing comics like Frank Randle to be huge in the north with no comparable success in the south. While someone like 'Chubby' Brown represents a regionally specific success story, a curiosity at best in the south, it isn't for reasons of dialect. Contemporary comic writers and performers can rarely sustain careers based on regional

exclusivity, while dialect levelling has in any case softened the linguistic
divide. There is more to the League's northern language than short
vowels, reduced definite articles (the pub the Swiss becomes not
't'Swiss', but just 'Swiss') and a few 'nowts' and 'Mams'. They
frequently offer what Bennett calls the 'laughter of recognition',[72] the
rhythms and quirks of everyday speech. Specific phrases might be either
recognisable or exotic for the viewer; Pauline dropping the 'sh' from the
word 'shit' ('the 'it on my shoes'), Geoff's use of the word 'bab' ('Hull
for crap', Shearsmith once explained), expressions like 'neither nowt nor
summat' or Iris's very particular use of the word 'lady' when verbally
savaging Judee.

The Importance of Being Egregious

The north assumes a 'masculine' identity in relation to the feminised
south, the land of 'angry young men' and 'blue' comedians. But there is
also a tradition, in Hoggart's working-class mums, *Coronation Street*,
Alan Bennett's writing, Victoria Wood, and Les Dawson's backstep
gossips, of equating the north with women who are 'survivors'. When
Roger Wilmut attributes Bennett's tragi-comedy to his regional
background, the latter equates the 'northern experience' with women; 'I
think it's just being northern – northern women's lives are slung between
three poles; dirt, disease and the lavatory. It is funny, but it's also sad.'[73]

The League often give us the north in drag, which produces a
more ambivalent image, cruel, caricatured, sometimes even misogynist.
To the accusation of misogyny (a word that the Gents have occasionally
used themselves on DVD commentaries), one could point to the
grossness of most of the male characters, but try applying that argument
to Benny Hill to see how convincing it is. One could also point to the
high number of female fans of the series, but speculate that most of them
are likely to be younger and more middle class than the Vasey women.
In any case, both of these responses deflect the question rather than
answering it. Several of the League's female characters conform to the

image of the 'tyrant', past her prime, sexually frustrated, 'libido in inverse proportion to her declining sexual appeal'.[74]

Pauline is the most complex of these figures, and certainly the most popular. In some ways, the initial Jobcentre sketches are the closest the series ever gets to social comment; one could imagine Pauline as a 'Thatcherite' monster in the alternative comedy era. But this is always in tension with a certain lairy misogyny that informs the character, equating aggressive women with sexually frustrated, aging lesbians. The battle-lines are firmly gendered – aren't there any unemployed women in Vasey? – but there are other social differences that add a layer of complexity to this *One Flew Over the Cuckoo's Nest* scenario. The richest of the early sketches is 'Egregious' (1.3), which not only offers a glimpse of redemptive vulnerability ('Love?'/'No ... there was somebody once'), but finds some real drama in the Pauline–Ross dynamic. Ross stands apart from his fellow jobseekers even before he is revealed as an internal investigator. He is educated and articulate, qualities that have the strange effect of making him less sympathetic. How different this battle might be if Ross resembled Phil Daniels's tricksterish, proletarian 'dole scum' in Mike Leigh's *Meantime* (Channel 4, 1983). 'It's a university now', snaps Dark Ross of series three when Pauline reminds him that he went to a polytechnic, but his education is an issue before that. Being the voice of reason doesn't always make you popular in comedy because it sometimes stands in opposition to the comedy generated by someone we wouldn't (or shouldn't) otherwise like. And who does Ross speak for anyway? Not Mickey, who he regards scornfully when Pauline bullies him out of going for a job interview (1.1). 'Egregious' stages a role-play session in which Ross 'interviews' Pauline for a job, and uses it as an opportunity to humiliate her. It ostensibly represents her comeuppance, particularly when she likens people to pens ('if they don't work, you chuck 'em away, bin 'em!'), but instead it signals the shift that future episodes will build on. Ross uses his education against Pauline, asking her if she's an egregious person, a word she doesn't recognise, introducing a class dimension into their battle. His belittling of her as both uneducated and 'too old, *Miss*' is no

55

'Beg me' – Ross enjoys his job a little too much

more cruel than anything she has said to her jobseekers, but the unruly dynamics of comedy make it less forgivable. The studio audience is delighted when she bounces back to demonstrate that actions are more powerful than words, beating him up with his clipboard. At the start of series two, Pauline's rehabilitation begins, replaced by the power-dressing nightmare Cathy Carter Smith. Fired from a literal McJob at the Burger Me takeaway, Pauline finds herself at Ross's mercy. 'Beg me', he tells her when she asks for his help getting her old job back (2.3). There's little sign that she's learned her lesson, but once again Ross seems like the bad guy. When Pauline returns in series three, we are invited to sympathise with her more fully, and Ross has become an outright villain, but the 'dyke and dildo' prison jokes are still sending out less generous signals.

In contrast with Pauline, Stella becomes less sympathetic over time. Charlie and Stella are a bickering couple, who conform to the convention Orwell detects in seaside postcards. 'Sex-appeal vanishes at about the age of twenty-five … . The amorous honeymooning couple reappear as the grim-visaged wife and shapeless, moustachioed, red-nosed husband, no intermediate stage being allowed for.'[75] Stella sports aggressively highlighted hair, her skin fag-ash grey and mottled with broken blood vessels that speak of perpetual disappointment and resentment that burns like stomach acid. Together, they are George and Mildred curdled into an unendurable cycle of spite and infrequent, bad sex, 'like shoving an oyster into a parking meter'. In an early sketch, included in the radio series and filmed but not broadcast as part of series one, Stella is allowed some glimmers of pathos. After flirting unsuccessfully with her daughter's boyfriend Tony (who will become her lover in later episodes), she encapsulates a lifetime of desperation in one line: 'We've never done owt – you learn Spanish!' As the series develops, Charlie becomes more sympathetic, Stella more monstrous. She is particularly vindictive in the Christmas Special, and an insatiable castrating harridan in series three, seen frequenting an amusement arcade called the Greedy Slits.

I don't wish to take up residence on the moral high ground here, and my discussion of Pauline should already have indicated the ambivalence at work in the League's gendered world. 'Ambivalence' might seem like a weak response, but it's at the heart of a lot of the most interesting comedy. We may not, and should not, want to give comedy a free pass to say what it wants, but we probably do need to come to terms with its unruly nature. The cross-dressing is particularly central to this question. A lot of Victoria Wood's comedy derives from older and/or not conventionally attractive female bodies, from snobbish, vitriolic, bullying women; it isn't a push to imagine some of the League's material (Judee and Iris, in particular) being performed by Wood and Julie Walters. The difference is, of course, that Wood also gives us female voices, both her authorial one and those of actors like Walters, Patricia Routledge and Susie Blake, whose bigoted TV announcer is effectively an upmarket Bernice. However, Laraine Porter provides another way of thinking about certain types of drag in comedy, as 'a fixation with aspects of femininity which are unknowable to men'.[76] Her shining example is Les Dawson and Roy Barraclough's Cissie and Ada, defined

by their over-the-fence gossip, hot flushes and 'hysterical-ectomies'.
One version of this male fixation on 'female trouble' in *The League of
Gentlemen* is expressed through the transgendered body of Barbara, a
'man' coming to terms with menstruation and the hormonal
rollercoaster of corporeal femininity. Like Tubbs, Barbara's 'insides are
all wrong'. A different version of anatomical drag, one that doesn't
hinge on gynaecological excess, is represented by Iris Krell, Judee
Levinson's brash cleaning lady. Porter identifies Cissie and Ada as
survivors, 'tough, unrefined and unattractive',[77] which makes Iris their
younger and more libidinous descendant, a connection visible in Gatiss's
repertoire of leers and gurning grimaces. With her bleached hair,
make-up seemingly applied in the dark, hairy mole on her cheek and
ruined teeth, Iris initially resembles some of the crueller stereotypes of
unattractive women in vulgar comedy. While her resigned 'Yes, Mrs
Levinson' underlines some of the limitations of her life, she is ultimately
empowered by her body and her appetites. She is vulgar and earthy,
recalling stealing 'fanny rag-bags from Primrose Valley' or regaling
Judee with rather too much information about her athletic love life with
husband Ron, 'this way, that way – some of it barely legal!' She gives
Alvin a conspiratorial leer, working the checkout in the supermarket
where Sunny has sent him to buy extra 'provisions' for their upcoming
Swingers' night (2.2). That both characters are played by Gatiss
underlines the contrast between the general disappointment and sense of
confinement felt by most Vasey inhabitants and someone who immerses
herself in physical pleasure (pissed on Malibu, skirt tucked into her
knickers) and can overturn power relations very effectively when the
upwardly mobile Judee crosses the line. There is a harsher world to
come back to – an uncomfortable scene shows Judee visiting Iris's home,
a hell of overflowing cat-litter trays and way too many children – but Iris
is nothing if not a survivor.

TV comedy often thrives in small worlds, and in many respects
Royston Vasey offers the sense of confinement that drives many a
sitcom. Comic versions of the 'Local' can be found in sitcoms as diverse
as the suburban obsessiveness of *Ever Decreasing Circles* (BBC1,

58

I Will Survive: Iris leers at Alvin

1984–7, 1989), *Father Ted*'s Craggy Island (Channel 4, 1995–8) and
another Local Shop-based series, *Open All Hours* (BBC2/BBC1, 1973,
1976–85). But in other ways, Vasey constitutes a large and complex
creation, encompassing different generic landscapes: the faded industrial
town of Kitchen Sink drama, the rural and the suburban.

59

Look Back in Anger

The three businessmen, Geoff, Mike and Brian, are the characters most
closely associated with Vasey's post-industrial townscape, and best
represent the more socially observed, less gothic, aspects of the series.
A sequence in episode 1.1 follows them from the factory, through
'bummer's alley' to the Mason's Arms pub, and thereafter in series one
we mostly meet them in pubs and restaurants. British realist drama is
often about upheavals in masculinity, 'angry' or otherwise, and Geoff is
a detailed portrait of male failure. As a line manager in a plastics factory
that might benefit from the New Road, Mike is a medium-sized fish in a
stagnant pond, while ineffectual Brian grew up on the Swanmills Estate.

If Geoff resents the latter for his comparatively 'spoilt' background, he despises the former for having achieved a modicum of success from the same beginnings that have brought him nothing but defeat. While he never captured T-shirt/slogan iconicity in the way that Pauline or Tubbs did, Geoff Tipps is one of the League's most enduring and rounded, yet critically overlooked, creations; Shearsmith fully inhabits him and emphasises the humanity within this volatile bundle of rage. Geoff resembles Bobby Ball after sleeping rough for a few weeks. He has little right to be sympathetic; one infers all manner of unspoken prejudices as well as his more personal resentments. And yet he approaches something like tragi-comedy. Like Harold Steptoe, Geoff is trapped not only by his grim surroundings but by his own limitations. Just as Harold had aspirations towards cultural elevation that would be thwarted by his lack of talent as much as his manipulative father, Geoff's comedy aspirations are doomed by his inability to tell a joke.

Geoff's defining sketch is 'Mau Mau' (1.1), which establishes his simultaneous attraction to and incomprehension of comedy. At the Indian restaurant Shebabs, he bullies Brian into telling Mike an Englishman/Irishman/Scotsman joke, which neither of them can

Industrial townscape: Mike, Geoff and Brian in 'bummer's alley'

properly remember. Geoff drives from the back seat – 'Do the voice', he interjects impatiently – but neither of them really know where they're going. Getting to the end of the joke becomes literally life or death when Geoff holds a gun to Mike's head as Brian stumbles at the punchline. On the face of it, 'Mau Mau' is among the more sketch-bound items from series one, shot 'fourth wall' style in a studio at Yorkshire Television, with a definite punchline (when a terrified Mike completes the joke, Geoff responds 'Oh, have you heard it?' and orders another round), and establishing the gun as a recurring device for easing Geoff's sketches towards their denouements. Taken in isolation, it may not seem especially character-driven. It's concerned with the mechanics of joke-telling, particularly those narrative-based jokes that circulate within social gatherings. Geoff loses his temper when Brian, in telling the joke, chooses a fruit that is too large because it disrupts the escalation built into the story; 'Mau Mau' refers to having an item of fruit anally inserted, so you can't introduce a banana too early. Mike casually tells Brian a punning gag as Geoff tries to remember the rest of the joke. A brief cutaway to the Dentons provides an ellipsis and, when we return, Geoff is lost in brow-furrowing concentration, trying to get 'Mau Mau' back on track as the other two have moved onto discussing the New Road. But there are already signs of a greater depth to the character as he tearfully recounts his childhood failure in a talent contest ('Me Mam said I would win – I was only eight!') Of the original sketches, the funniest and darkest is the Best Man speech Geoff delivers at Mike's wedding (1.5). Dressed as a court jester, Geoff's initially good-natured jibes at the groom turn predictably ugly as he recounts their 'friendship' in resentfully competitive terms. Within a catalogue of real or imagined defeats, he can only find one petty, vicious little victory:

61

> Oh, but it's here that things finally went in my favour because in '87 both of our Mums got really ill roughly at the same time. Mine, thank God, she got better, but yours died, didn't she, Mike? *Didn't she!?* Yeah, your Mum died and mine didn't – I won that! At least I won the Mums!

Failed clown: Geoff tries to remember 'Mau Mau'

62

'I won the Mums' — Geoff's best man speech

Vasey's more sympathetic characters often resemble children, like Tubbs wishing for a new dress as a shooting star goes by. Over three series, Geoff never really stops being the eight-year-old boy promised success and granted the most abject of defeats. He even has the attention span of a child: after telling everyone how much he hates Mike and once more

pulling his gun, he launches into the wedding toast as though nothing
has happened.

Series two gives the businessmen more of a storyline, albeit
confined to two episodes, freeing them from both the sketch format and
the studio set. On their way to a plastics convention, they get lost in the
woods, *Blair Witch*-meets-*Deliverance* style. The story builds on
another misplaced aspiration. Too fat to join the army, Geoff did a stint
in the Territorial Army and goes 'native', smearing dirt on his face and
fixing his tie around his head. He nearly kills Mike and Brian is injured
during an ill-advised river crossing. Geoff has a moment of insight –
'This job I'm doing now, I'm no good at it' – but once again pins his
redemption on a task that he doesn't seem quite up to. 'If I can get us
back to that hotel in front of that board – hopefully with you still alive –
then maybe I'll have done something', he tells Brian. Against all the
odds, and particularly Geoff's capacity for endangering his 'friends', all
three make it to the convention. The storyline confirms Geoff's potential

Missing in action: Geoff goes 'native'

for greater character development. Wherever he goes, including London in series three, he takes his 'trap' with him. But his series two misadventures also play on the liminality of Vasey, never very far from the perilous countryside.

'We Didn't Burn Him!'

Nothing else in *The League of Gentlemen* caught the popular imagination quite like Tubbs, Edward and the Local Shop. According to Stuart Maconie, the series' most lasting impact lay in changing the meaning of the word 'Local'. ' "Local" doesn't mean quite near where you live any more. "Local" now means weird and sinister. They've changed the meaning of a word in the English language.'[78] The word branded the show to such an extent that *On the Town* became marked retrospectively by a strange sense of absence. And yet their absence from Spent makes perfect sense, given that it is in some ways a more integrated town than the Royston Vasey that appeared on TV. The inhabitants of Spent mingle a bit more than they would in the first two TV series, less constrained by the potential problem of having a performer interact with too many versions of himself; there are social gatherings on Bonfire Night and at Christmas that might have been harder to realise on screen.[79] On radio, the rural aspects of the show are largely confined to Chinnery, who travels between town and country; an important referent here is long-running rural radio soap *The Archers* (Radio 4, 1951–). On television, the Local Shop feels less a part of Vasey than a world in its own right. It has its own language ('twelvety', 'I can, I can't') and economy, which doesn't depend on them selling anything. The 'precious things', none more evocative than the snow globes, have no exchange value, functioning instead as magical totems ('He covets the precious things of the shop'). In dialogue cut from episode 1.1, this self-sustaining economy is given pagan overtones as it parodies *The Wicker Man* (1973); 'Strangers make the crops fail … . If the crops fail the town fails.'

It's well documented that the Tattsyrups were inspired by an encounter with a suspicious shopkeeper in Rottindgean. But to this real life Local Shop and *The Wicker Man*, one must add a less direct influence. In 1994, the police dug up the backyard of 25 Cromwell Street, Gloucester. The house's owners, Fred and Rosemary West, were subsequently convicted of the murders of twelve young women and girls, among them lodgers, former partners and their own abused children. 'You'll never leave' had been considered as Gloucester's tourist slogan, as though ghastly comedy was determined to seep out of this atrocity. Most serial killers give rise to waves of sick jokes, but the Wests' physiognomies and provincial depravity (they were Local murderers) seemed to attract it particularly. *Viz* teamed Fred with the serial killer GP Harold Shipman as 'Harold and Fred (They Make Ladies Dead)', and mocked up an ad for a commemorative Teddy Bear, 'Little Ted West'. The Wests pervade the League's conception of the grimly comic, the unspeakable and the 'Local', from Tubbs and Edward to Pauline's Exocet (supposedly the name of Rosemary's vibrator) and Alvin burying bodies under his patio. Rosemary is supposed to have once answered the door wearing the slippers of one missing girl, like Tubbs in her victim's hiking boots. Fred West's physical appearance seems to have amused and appalled equally: 'he looked like an intermediate stage in the transformation of man into werewolf', according to one description.[80] Curly haired, often described as 'simian', there are visual traces of Fred in Geoff and Pop (another terrifying landlord with unspeakable designs on his tenants). The Dentons bear some resemblance to the Wests, too, embodying the suburban family home that Benjamin will 'never leave'. 'God forgive me for saying it', Dyson told one interviewer, 'but there is something terribly comic in the situation of suburban murderers, even though the reality is too horrific to contemplate.'[81] *The League of Gentlemen* affords some comic distance from a 'reality too horrific to contemplate'. Its victims are predominantly male, and its most prolific serial killers are shifted to another 'primitive' locale that modernity has left behind.

65

In its most restricted, uncanny and forbidding sense, the Local maps onto the bleak rural landscape, magnifying (even unbalancing) its presence in the series. The very first shot of episode 1.1 presents us with an image that might be idyllic if it were not for the heavy clouds hanging ominously above it, a 'James Herriot' landscape, or the peaceful countryside about to have a bomb dropped on it in *The Comic Strip Presents* logo. *The League of Gentlemen* draws on the two most enduring generic images of the countryside, the 'savage or beastly' landscape,[82] and the pastoral 'essence' of the nation. The former tends to be associated more with British film than television, particularly with movies like *Straw Dogs* (1971), *The Wicker Man* and *An American Werewolf in London* (1981); Tubbs and Edward might have been at home in the latter's unfriendly pub, the Slaughtered Lamb. But there is a rural gothic tradition on television, too, in Nigel Kneale's work for example, from various incarnations of *Quatermass*, to the 'Baby' episode of *Beasts* (ATV, 1976), where the witch suckling a gruesome familiar might now make us think of Tubbs and her piglet. More recently, an episode of *Torchwood* gave a particularly evocative title, 'Countrycide', to the tale of a community of cannibals in the Brecon Hills (BBC3, 2006). As Peter Hutchings puts it, 'country folk are … sometimes revealed as decidedly primitive and altogether too close to nature, with rural traditions involving a deeply unhealthy insularity and stasis'.[83] The Local equates not only with insularity ('There's nothing for you here') and anachronism ('I was in a war'), but incest. Pig snouts and son David's hirsute body might make us suspect that bestiality figures somewhere in the Tattsyrup family line, too, while the revelation of Hilary Briss's wife as a cow extends the overfamiliarity with nature, as well as adding a further transgressive mystique to the Special Stuff.

The other representation of the countryside has been a particular mainstay of primetime British television, whether in sitcoms like *Last of the Summer Wine* and *The Vicar of Dibley* (BBC1, 1994–) or nostalgic Sunday-night soothers like *Heartbeat* (Yorkshire, 1992–). The most blatant referent in *The League of Gentlemen* is *All Creatures Great and Small* (BBC1, 1977–80, 1990), based on the autobiographical

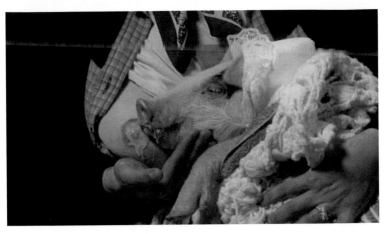

Too close to nature: Tubbs suckles a pig

books of former vet James Herriot, which had already been adapted into two films. Chinnery is described as 'a Peter Davison-like vet',[84] although Davison's Tristan had been a rather more rakish character than Christopher Timothy's clean-cut James. We sometimes see Chinnery cycling through an idealised rural landscape, at one point dragging a dead dog whose lead has got entangled in his wheels. The sketches, *Fast Show*-like in their enjoyable repetition, trade on Gatiss's resemblance to Davison, who he kidnapped (abetted by David Walliams) in a sketch for the BBC's 1999 *Doctor Who Night*. A supporting regular character in *All Creatures*, Miss Pumphrey, has a pampered dog Tricky Woo in whose name she is constantly calling James out to treat minor or nonexistent canine complaints. Chinnery takes symbolic, and entirely unwitting, revenge on Herriot's behalf on a Mrs De Courcey and Bentley, the dog rendered flatulent by a diet of poached salmon, *foie gras* and truffles. Bentley lets forth a deadly fart during a rectal examination that propels him onto an open fire, and a second emission proves literally explosive, showering vet and lady of leisure with blood and entrails (2.4). Chinnery functions much like *The Comic Strip*'s bomb, then, if with the best of intentions.

67

Herriot's revenge: Mrs De Courcey and Chinnery witness Bentley's fate

Rural Horror: Farmer Tinsel visits his 'scarecrow'

The intermediary between the countryside of Chinnery and that of the Local Shop is Farmer Tinsel, ostensibly a character designed to receive 'upsetting news' from the vet (putting the wrong dog to sleep, attempting to deliver a calf from a cow's rectum). The cruellest vision of the rural landscape involves Tinsel's revenge on his wife's lover, Andrew,

The 'savage' landscape: Chloe, Radclyffe, 'scarecrow' and Tinsel

keeping him imprisoned as a scarecrow in the loneliest of fields. The
sketch had been used in *On the Town*, which included a follow-up in
which Chloe and Radclyffe Denton trap their headmistress as their own
'special' scarecrow.[85] The macabre humour derives from Andrew
managing to alert the Denton twins while Tinsel allows him a brief
respite from his hood, only to discover that they have always known the
real identity of their 'special friend'. They replace the hood and skip off
gleefully. Two worlds combine here: the beastly countryside is rarely
more chilling, but these monstrous children have emerged from a rather
more 'suburban' environment.

69

Chez Denton, Chez Levinson

The words 'Royston Vasey' and 'suburban' may not seem to have an
immediate affinity, but the Oxford English dictionary offers two
definitions of 'suburban', not only the literal socio-geographic one, but
also as 'having only limited interests and narrow-minded views'. Such a
definition arises out of popular culture's love–hate relationship with the

Showcase suburban lawn:
the Dentons' toad topiary

'Feminine' spaces and class war:
Judee's fitted kitchen

Judee's pissing cherub ...

... and Iris's pissing boy

suburbs, producing a set of images familiar from sitcoms, movies and pop music: upward mobility, snobbery, showcase frontages to otherwise uniform houses, competitive squabbles with neighbours, sexual perversity behind a veneer of middle-class respectability.[86] In *The League of Gentlemen*, suburban imagery is condensed into Swanmills Estate, the 'nice' part of town where we find the Dentons' 'Toad Hall', with its batrachian topiary on the lawn, and Judee Levinson, with her spacious fitted kitchen and pissing cherub in the front garden (nicely counterpointed with an actual pissing boy outside Iris's flats.) It also seems to be the pristine location in which Papa Lazarou begins his wife-napping activities.

The Dentons are the suburban counterparts to Tubbs and Edward's rural perversity, similarly over-intimate with animals, harbouring terrible designs on their nephew, and spawning monstrous offspring. They are equally misshapen, too: in his gigantic underpants, crotch aimed threateningly at Benjamin, Harvey resembles something you might see in a medieval carnival. Their obsession with hygiene and order puts me in mind of anthropologist Mary Douglas's definition of dirt as 'matter out of place': 'Where there is dirt there is a system. Dirt is the by-product of a systematic ordering and classification of matter, in so far as ordering involves rejecting inappropriate elements.'[87]

This ordering extends from the house, with its plethora of brushes, towels, locks, separate toilet rolls labelled '1's' and '2's', to Benjamin's body, constantly policed for signs of self-abuse ('cavorting with Madame Palm and her five lovely daughters') or passing 'solids' into the wrong lavatory. Taboos surrounding cleanliness are fearful of margins, the borders of the body and abject substances. When Douglas cites stickiness/viscosity as 'an aberrant fluid or a melting solid',[88] it's hard not to think of Harvey's grossest euphemism for masturbation as spraying 'sticky white love piss'. But if 'dirt' grows out of a system, it can also be reclassified. Semen may be 'a persistent stain', but urine can be recycled as 'aqua vitae', Harvey downing a pint glass of his own piss before a horrified Benjamin at breakfast (1.3). The Dentons' perversity grows out of a combination of amphibian empathy and a particularly unsavoury *Health and Efficiency* outlook; Benjamin finds a magazine

71

Classifying matter: Harvey, Benjamin and toilet rolls

Reclassifying bodily fluids: Harvey pours a glass of aqua vitae

called *Women with Toads* in a drawer in his bedroom. In series two, they become the more malign figures of the radio series. When they trick Benjamin into answering the door naked, it isn't clear whether they really do have a 'Nude Day' or if it's just another method of psychological torture. They meet the same fate as in *On the Town*, imprisoned in their own amphibarium, Harvey 'hoist by my own pet toad' but actually eliminated by his own children.

Judee manifests suburbia as a 'feminine' space, the snobbish descendant of *The Good Life*'s Margo (BBC1, 1975–8) and *Keeping Up Appearances*' Hyacinth Bucket/Bouquet (BBC1, 1990–5). What starts out as the verbal torture of her cleaner, Iris ('you must feel like a little Rwandan let loose in Harrods' food hall') turns out to be a two-way sado-masochistic game, even though Judee seems to get the best of most of their early bouts of class warfare. Iris comes out on top when she introduces the topic of unruly bodies into Mrs Levinson's sterile abode: her own sexual activity, and particularly Judee's daughter's eating disorder. 'We never knew which end it was going to come out of', she recalls, cackling gleefully. Here, too, 'dirt' haunts the spotless suburban home, as Iris cheerfully remembers 'Morrisons' bags full of sick' discovered behind ceiling tiles (2.4). Things come to a head as Judee relishes her collection of hotel soaps while Iris scrubs the toilet. Mrs Levinson goes a little far when she likens Ron to a 'shaved monkey in a tracksuit', and the proverbial Marigolds are off: 'Thinking you're summat when you're nowt. You deluded dried up old witch! With hot flushes and not even a buzzing Philips Ladyshave between your legs to keep you company on a cold winter's night. I pity you, lady!' (2.6). Framed in distraught proximity to the camera, Iris clutching a threatening toilet brush, Judee's demolition is comprehensive and final, her own body invoked against her. In *On the Town*, they end on a conciliatory note: the score is one-all and they'll play for best of three, clinking glasses ('Cheers'). The final episode of series two adds a further twist to their perverse relationship. 'Oh, Mum!' cries Judee, collapsing into Iris's arms. Iris's victory can only be won by slaying the menopausal dragon, but the nature of the 'game' and its unexpectedly emotional outcome (the studio audience applaud the hug as though it's some kind of 'feelgood' reconciliation) tempers the cruelty of Judee's verbal assassination.

Where series one was open-ended, series two has more of a sense of closure, with the apparent death of both Tubbs and Edward and

73

Game over: Iris triumphs over her employer

the Dentons, Hilary's escape to the Caribbean, Benjamin's final
liberation, Pauline's arrest for kidnapping Ross, and Judee and Iris's
rapprochement. There is also, with the benefit of hindsight, a degree of
closure to *The League of Gentlemen* as a sketch-based show, the
culmination of a process that had refined and adapted live material,
moving across different media, adding new material and establishing the
parameters of Royston Vasey, but mainly building on material that had
emerged on stage. From here on, the League would work almost entirely
with new material developed specifically for television, the Christmas
Special marking a new beginning. In this respect, the 'Special Stuff'
hinted at what was to come, with its greater emphasis on narrative
development. In the short term, it also represented the growing presence
of horror in the series. The night-time opening scene of 2.1 cuts between
Benjamin's escape from the Local Shop, David's monstrous shape
looming in the window and a cart pulled by black plumed horses and
manned by a mysterious figure in a top hat cracking a whip. This was
the first appearance of Papa Lazarou, a character who features
prominently in the next chapter, which explores the interplay between
the comic, the gothic and the uncanny.

74

4 Pandemonium Carnival

In a piece written for the *Independent on Sunday* in 2000, Jeremy Dyson reiterated one of the League's formative influences:

> It's true that we share a love of horror films. Although we didn't meet until our college years, there are moments we can locate in our collective childhoods that we all shared. On 5 November 1975 I saw *Carry on Screaming* for the first time. Both Mark and Reece can remember watching the same screening, both terrified and tickled by the spectre of Oddbod Junior.[89]

It's possible that this is a tale to file under 'apocryphal'. Certainly, it exists in different versions: sometimes the year is 1976, sometimes Pemberton is included in this synchronised viewing, sometimes not. When I interviewed Dyson, he only seemed confident that he and Gatiss had seen it on the same night, but rightly pointed out that in the three-channel 70s, people were more likely to have seen the same things on TV. No matter. It's an irresistible story, and I've found myself speculating whether I was tuned in too. It has taken on the status of an origin story, framing their relationship with horror (and comedy) in terms of collective memory. Give or take variations in ethnicity and sexuality, the League members seem to have led oddly synchronised childhoods, in which fantasy, horror and magic played key roles; all four possessed the Dick Smith Horror Make-Up Kit. But the story underlines another important point. The League are (accurately) characterised as film buffs, but most of their formative influences, including horror movies, seem to have been experienced via television.

References to cult horror proliferate in *The League of Gentlemen*. *The Wicker Man* is the most frequently cited. Gatiss's Scottish policeman meets a fate similar to Edward Woodward's when he investigates the Local Shop (1.1), and series three includes a pub called the Salmon of Knowledge and the creepy-funny moment where Mike's car alarm prompts the residents of Geoff's tower block to pop up from behind a wall like the inhabitants of Summerisle (3.3). Interestingly, there's very little Hammer among the League's horror references. The British gothic excavated in the series is mainly that of mavericks and one-offs like *Don't Look Now* and *Theatre of Blood* (both 1973), or rival studios like Tigon and Amicus. Amicus takes on a particular importance in relation to the Christmas Special's portmanteau structure. The studio is remembered primarily for a cycle that began with *Dr Terror's House of Horrors* (1964). *From beyond the Grave* (1973) is particularly important, with its 'Local Shop' framing story, and the opening line spoken by Peter Cushing's northern antiques shopkeeper, 'Can I help you at all?' Gatiss chose *From beyond the Grave* as his favourite horror film in the collection *Cinema Macabre*.[90] There are other reasons why Amicus might be a congenial source for recent TV comedies like the League and the note-perfect Steve Coogan vehicle *Dr Terrible's House of Horrible* (BBC2, 2001). In contrast with the Manichean gothic of Hammer, Peter Hutchings characterises Amicus as 'cynical, sardonic, cruel, modern',[91] the punishments inflicted on erring characters ridiculously disproportionate to their crimes. Helen Wheatley, on the other hand, suggests that Amicus points to the permeable divide between film and TV horror, the portmanteau format on film easily blurring into the anthology format that has characterised a lot of gothic television (*Mystery and Imagination* [ITV, 1966–70], *Tales of the Unexpected* [ITV, 1979–88], *Hammer House of Horror* [ITV, 1980]).[92] The League had their first stab at Amicus-style horror in their home movie *Highgate House of Horror* (1995), which affords a rare opportunity to see Dyson act alongside his fellow Gents.[93]

The mixture of horror and comedy on TV can be traced back to US gothic sitcoms like *The Addams Family* (ABC, 1964–8) and *The Munsters* (MCA, 1964–6, 1988–91), where the juxtaposition of the monstrous and the normatively suburban has sometimes been seen as a parody of postwar American values.[94] The 'neighbours from hell' format could be seen as a precursor to Tubbs and Edward and the Dentons (who conflate suburban respectability with the monstrous). But in mixing the two genres in such a conspicuously cultish way, the League suggest that a more telling point of comparison would be contemporaneous shows like *Dr Terrible's House of Horrible* and *Garth Marenghi's Dark Place* (Channel 4, 2003). *Dr Terrible* built each episode around a specific subgenre of British horror. 'And Now the Fearing' parodied Amicus directly, 'Frenzy of Tongs' wedded Sax Rohmer to *Doctor Who*'s 'The Talons of Weng Chiang',[95] while 'Lesbian Vampire Lovers of Lust' probably speaks for itself. *Dr Terrible*'s disappointing ratings suggest that it might have been *too* cultish, its jokes dependent on knowing one's lesbian vampire trilogies or being able to recognise 70s' icons like Sheila Keith and Oliver Tobias. *Garth Marenghi* meanwhile sought to do for low-budget sci-fi horror what Victoria Wood's 'Acorn Antiques' did for teatime soaps. Its gags grew out of a mixture of lovingly simulated ineptitude and the deluded hubris of its eponymous (but fictional) creator, 'author, dreamweaver, visionary, plus actor'. While the League (and their fans) can play spot-the-reference, but rarely rely on that solely for the joke, their channelling of horror largely goes beyond pure pastiche or parody to create a genuinely disturbing world of their own. For at least one viewer (responding to the Christmas Special), the horror took the programme out of the realm of the comic altogether: 'This isn't funny, it scared the hell out of me.'[96]

Horror and fantasy are writ particularly large on the CVs of two of the Gents. Mark Gatiss and Jeremy Dyson have both written books and essays on horror cinema. Dyson has adapted Robert Aickman's 'strange tales' across different media,[97] including directing the short film *The Cicerones* for Film 4 (2000), which would sit nicely in any revival of the BBC's 'Ghost Story for Christmas'. Some of Dyson's own short stories display the influence of writers like Aickman and Ramsey Campbell, while Gatiss's *Doctor Who* scripts have played particularly to the Gothic aspects of that series. Perhaps most revealingly, Dyson, Gatiss and Shearsmith provided a commentary for the DVD of *Blood on Satan's Claw* as part of the Tigon boxed set. The *Satan's Claw* commentary works at three levels. First, there are attempts at analysis, albeit primarily at the level of fannish detail: Gatiss obsessing over the film's many links to *Doctor Who* (Wendy Padbury, Anthony Ainley, Roberta Tovey). Second, it offers what fans have come to expect of commentaries by the League, a combination of comedy and mediated intimacy. And so we are treated to schoolboy irreverence about the film ('How many of those children are under thirty-five?'), Gatiss's Patrick Wymark impersonations, and anecdotes that seem to take us back to Royston Vasey, like Dyson's childhood memory of a mysterious figure decapitating telegraph poles with a chainsaw on the outer edges of Leeds. Third, and again tying in with the 'intimacy effect', the League continually evoke the memory of watching the film (and other British horrors) as part of 'Appointment with Fear', the regional seasons of horror films on ITV that followed *News at Ten* on a Friday in the 1970s. Within this Friday-night subculture, 'Appointment with Fear' might be consumed alongside generously illustrated books by Alan Frank or Denis Gifford, offering tantalising stills that intensified the anticipation for particular titles to materialise in TV listings magazines.[98] 'What was your one that you never saw?' asks Gatiss at one point, a resonant question for horror fans of a particular generation. The cumulative effect of the commentary is precisely of watching a classic horror film on a Friday night with the most entertaining friends possible.

There is, of course, a danger of overemphasising the importance of horror in *The League of Gentlemen* at the expense of other aspects of the programme, and yet its gothic qualities and film-buff referentiality undoubtedly intensified the cult appeal of the series. Horror accounts for the loose story arcs in the first two series, with Tubbs and Edward's resistance to the New Road bringing rural horror to the fore and the 'Special Stuff' both taking series two in a more graphic direction and alluding to things that could not be represented. In particular, the first two series are anchored in two monstrous families, the Dentons and the Tattsyrups. As Benjamin passes between these two unhomely places, a gothicised suburbia and the Local Shop, he starts to resemble the gothic TV heroine identified by Helen Wheatley, removed from a place of safety and trapped within a domestic space that has become threatening and imprisoning.[99]

The Idiot's Lantern: Uncanny Television

Even lower in the televisual food chain than reality TV, list shows have few defenders. Nevertheless, *100 Greatest Scary Moments* (Channel 4, 2003) is, dare I say it, the masterpiece of the genre, its brilliance lying in it not being confined by generic categories. In her book on gothic television, Helen Wheatley gestures towards the larger category of 'Uncanny TV', located in those moments 'in which the familiar conventions of television are made strange'.[100] Wheatley has in mind moments specifically *within* the gothic and the fantastic, but *100 Greatest Scary Moments* suggests that Uncanny TV might be a more generically promiscuous category, one that includes not only horror, fantasy and the 'feel-bad historical', but public-information films, comedy, children's programmes, music videos, commercials and dubbed versions of European folk tales. The League figured prominently in the programme, both as fanboy pundits and as part of this legacy. In other words, they were presented as both having been shaped by and already having become part of the cultural memory of Uncanny TV. As Wheatley puts it:

> they acknowledge that domestic viewing of the horror genre produced a lasting effect on its audience, whereby the child crouching behind the sofa, transfixed by late-night horror television, becomes the knowing, adult producer and viewer twenty or thirty years later.[101]

79

Indeed, Gatiss seems to speak of the Christmas Special in terms of this dual identity:

> If I hadn't had anything to do with that and I'd turned on I'd have been as
> happy as Larry because it would just push all my buttons, in terms of the
> gorgeous Christmassiness, the Victorian setting, the silliness, and then the
> kind of spookiness as well.

The League's Christmas Special came in at number 24 in *Scary Moments* (although, admittedly, empirical precision is not the hallmark of these programmes), slightly more scary than *Buffy the Vampire Slayer*'s 'Hush' episode, but apparently not quite as terrifying as *The Wizard of Oz*. According to the Channel 4 website, the League had produced 'perhaps the most terrifying comedy series ever made'.[102] In *Scary Moments*' opening montage, Papa Lazarou, an itinerant carnival owner in minstrel blackface who accumulates 'wives', took his place alongside some more established monsters: Jason, Freddie and Leatherface, Jack Nicholson with his axe, Davros with his Daleks. *Scary Moments* speaks to, and of, a generation that grew up in the 1970s, a decade which has been remembered as a Golden Age for fantastic children's television. *Doctor Who* would hit a peak of consistency, from Jon Pertwee's earthbound invasion narratives to the high gothic of Tom Baker's early stories. At ITV's West Country/Wales franchise HTV, a strange convergence of the uncanny and the New Age culminated in *Children of the Stones* (1977), described in *Scary Moments* as '*The Wicker Man* for kids'. With its standing stones, ley-lines and creepy villagers, *Children* distilled its 'You'll Never Leave' narrative into a teatime format that left its mark on a generation. There were even ghostly comedies like *Rentaghost* (BBC) and *The Ghosts of Motley Hall* (HTV) (both starting in 1976), the latter, like *Children of the Stones*, featuring Freddie Jones, a virtual icon of children's fantasy TV and, appropriately, Mr Purblind in the League's Christmas Special. Public-information films shown on TV could go for the horror jugular even more aggressively. In 'Lonely Water' (1973), we might as well be in one of the BBC's M. R. James adaptations as the camera tracks across a misty pond to find a cowled figure, voiced unforgettably by Donald Pleasence, luring foolhardy children to a watery death. As Gatiss puts it in *Scary Moments* (Lonely *Water'* at number 75), 'the creepiness used to linger even into *Magpie*'. 'Play Safe – Kites and Planes' (1979) is part of a series warning of the dangers of electricity pylons and overhead wires, with a dead child guaranteed in every film. As a kite catches in the overhead wires with terrible consequences, it's hard not to suspect that 'Play Safe' influenced one of the League's Chinnery sketches (2.6), which cross-breeds *Kes* with the public-information film's evocation of death lurking in the countryside.

In its combination of the nostalgic and the macabre, *Scary Moments* positioned the League between the two polarised ways in which television often gets conceptualised as a medium for terror, one in which the domesticity of the medium protects the viewer from fear and one in which its status as what Jeffrey Sconce calls 'haunted media', a portal to phantasmatic worlds, intensifies the uncanny.[103] The early days of TV ownership were accompanied by sensational tales of ghostly faces that refused to depart from the screen, and a widespread perception of TV as a 'living presence' (and not necessarily a friendly one). Gatiss's *Doctor Who* story 'The Idiot's Lantern' (BBC1, 2006) revisits these fears in their original historical moment, the new technology that resembles an alien presence. An entity called the Wire consumes its viewers even as it masquerades as an RP-voiced BBC announcer. The story is set in 1953, a year that refers to two models of early television, the 'window on the world' represented by the Coronation (the epochal TV event exploited by the Wire) and an unspoken, but palpable reference to the Ur-text of British uncanny TV, *The Quatermass Experiment* (BBC1, 1953).[104] *Quatermass*'s impact was founded precisely on the idea that watching it at home intensified fear rather than alleviating it.[105] The notion of 'uncanny comedy' complicates things further. As a television comedy remembered for macabre chills as much as its jokes and catchphrases, *The League of Gentlemen* personifies the unresolved tension between the 'Local' (the domestic, the familiar, the comic) and the Uncanny.

The Uncanny, the Grotesque and the Comic

Like Wheatley, my understanding of the uncanny relies on Freud's
definition. Tracing the etymology of the word '*unheimlich*', he discerns
two meanings. *Heimlich* means both homely/familiar and something
that has been covered up or hidden. Its opposite, therefore, conveys a
feeling of the 'unhomely' (sometimes in a way that we can't quite put
our finger on) and something that has been hidden which now returns.
This 'something' – for Freud, an infantile anxiety or desire – returns in
disguise (as a ghost, a vampire, a terrifying house), so that the uncanny
represents the return of the repressed.[106] 'Uncanny television', therefore,
blurs the line between the homely and the unhomely; as Matthew Sweet
says of classic *Doctor Who*, 'it made you feel unsafe in your own
home'.[107] Watching the Daleks (or in my case, the Yeti on the London
Underground) from behind the sofa at one level seems to represent the
ne plus ultra of the home being simultaneously terrifying and offering a
place of precarious safety. But it is also undeniably a nostalgic evocation
of pleasurable fear, something that the horror-fantasy fan longs to return
to, or (as Wheatley suggests of the League) recreate in a more
sophisticated, knowing form. Nostalgia is sometimes defined as a kind
of 'homesickness', which would appear to cast it as diametrically
opposed to the uncanny. In any case, while nostalgia might account for
some of the gothic qualities in *The League of Gentlemen*, it doesn't
account for all of them. To the 'Local' and the uncanny, we need to add
a third term, the grotesque.

There are many different models for understanding the
grotesque, but when it comes to discussions of gross and vulgar comedy,
one of them has been especially influential. It is a measure of the grip
that Mikhail Bakhtin's theories of the 'carnivalesque' have on such
writing that one feels compelled to explain his ideas in order to justify
not using them. In *Rabelais and His World*, Bakhtin celebrates the
carnival of the middle ages as liberating and empowering, resistant to
elite culture and overturning hierarchies of authority, at least for a
day.[108] Part of this resistance involves an embrace of the grossness of the

body, privileging the mouth, the genitals and the bowels. While Bakhtin saw carnival as being historically and culturally specific, these ideas have been applied by many writers (this one included) to modern popular culture, ranging from low comedy to game shows to horror movies. We can't entirely ignore such ideas when considering a series whose two most popular characters have porcine features, one of whose 'insides are all wrong', and who eat hair sandwiches and dips made from (presumably their own) shit. Tubbs and Edward inspired an affection in their audience that suggests an embrace of the gross and the abject, but generally speaking, the grotesque body is not liberating in *The League of Gentlemen*. If anything, as Peter Hutchings argues, it's closer to 'body horror'.[109] Ultimately, the 'carnivalesque' only gets us so far, and takes us down an overfamiliar road. Another approach is needed.

According to Michael Steig, the grotesque is 'the managing of the uncanny by the comic'.[110] Following a broadly psychoanalytic approach, he links the grotesque, the uncanny and the comic to the managing of infantile impulses and anxieties, the uncanny offering the weakest defence and the comic offering the strongest. The grotesque manifests a 'double paradox': 'it at once allays and intensifies the effect of the uncanny; in pure comedy, at the other end of the spectrum from the uncanny, the defence is complete, and detachment is achieved'.[111] One might question the degree to which comedy represents a 'complete defence', unless one also considers Bergson's 'momentary anaesthesia of the heart'. Nevertheless, there is something useful about the notion of the grotesque that diverts threatening material 'in the direction of harmlessness without completely attaining it',[112] especially given that, once again, we are in 'a state of unresolved tension'.[113] Steig arrives at two 'extreme' kinds of grotesque, one that attempts a liberation from inhibition, and one that attempts a liberation from fear. The former would again explain the effect of the 'grossout', the mixture of disgust and delight that greets the spectacle of gross bodily functions: Bentley the dog exploding, or Tubbs feeding a worm to a bird. William Paul seems to have something similar in mind when he suggests that 'gross-out explicitly acknowledges the attractive in the repellent, the

83

beautiful in the ugly'.[114] However, if we really want to examine the dark heart of *The League of Gentlemen*, and consider the managing of the uncanny by the comic, we need to visit the circus.

Something Wicked This Way Comes: Primal Papa

In the ersatz suburbia of the Swanmills Estate, the shadow of a top-hatted figure looms over a white garage door. The ringed fingers of a sinister hand smear dirt on an equally white front door as it strikes the knocker. A housewife opens the door, and a figure in minstrel blackface, sporting a top hat, bandanna and a long leather coat, stares at her blankly. He is accompanied by a gypsy woman in a shawl, Mama Lazarou, and a three-legged dog. He switches on a less than reassuring grin, giving her and us the full benefit of his gold tooth, and in a voice simultaneously lisping and guttural, utters what will become the first, more deceptively benign, of his two catchphrases, 'Hello, Dave?' They establish that she *isn't* Dave and that no one called Dave lives there, but Lazarou won't let it go and continues to call her by the name that he will give to all of his wives. She tries to keep him out of the house, but unlike Dracula, Lazarou does not require permission to enter and he is soon inside, kicking the door open and breaking the security chain. The housewife attempts to mobilise the sort of well-rehearsed language that might come from a Neighbourhood Watch leaflet – 'You're intruding on my property. I'm going to have to ask you to leave' – but she's in *his* world now. Papa insists that he has 'pegs belonging to you', talks in non-sequiturs ('This is just a saga now!') and outright gibberish, and there's some business about a blockage in her toilet. The blackface adds another disturbing quality, as though he is the return of the repressed of light entertainment.[115] While he is in the bathroom, Mama Lazarou pleads for help and claims to have no idea who her husband is; he once came to her house just as he is doing now. She confirms that the strange language they speak is made up, but utters a dire warning, 'Don't make him angry – he can *do* things.' When Papa returns, materialising

84

unnervingly at her shoulder, the housewife attempts to simulate his strange language and finds herself worryingly understood and initiated into a deranged world that Lazarou seems to be forever improvising around himself. He delivers the most disturbing catchphrase in British comedy, 'You're *my* wife now!' and she nods in resignation, as though she always knew he was coming for her. The scene is from 'Destination: Royston Vasey' (2.1), which opens with the arrival of Papa Lazarou's Pandemonium Carnival, with equal nods to Tod Browning and Ray Bradbury (the Pandemonium Carnival is from *Something Wicked This Way Comes*). Papa has two setpieces in the episode. One of them comprises his circus act as an ineptly unconvincing medium, a sketch that dates back to *This Is It!*, where the act was performed by Mr Asmodeus. The 'You're my wife now' scene originated in the Highgate shows just before series one, where Lazarou emerged as the character we encounter in the TV series. It might be stretching a point to see Mr Asmodeus and Papa Lazarou as the same character, but it's hard to resist. The demon Asmodeus has his origins in Persian mythology, but his most resonant incarnations for our purposes can be found in Judaism. In the non-canonical 'Book of Tobit', Asmodai desires Sarah and murders a series of her suitors on their wedding night before they can consummate their relationship. In the Talmud, he is a more benign figure, but one with an eye for the ladies (and, more specifically, King Solomon's wives). But if Lazarou can be seen as having a mythological origin, he has a more mundane one, too, from which his more comic attributes seem to derive. Peter Papalazarou was apparently the name of a former landlord to Shearsmith and Pemberton, the character's phrases based on his mystifying phone calls. His two catchphrases underline the two dimensions of Lazarou. 'Hello, Dave?' finds the absurd in everyday speech, while 'You're my wife now' (which was presumably *not* something their landlord said) points to the mythological, the primal and the demonic.

85

The comic enactment of what is effectively a home-invasion narrative is what seems to have imprinted Papa on popular memory, not to mention T-shirts, posters and mobile ring tones. While less of a

crossover figure than Tubbs or Pauline, Lazarou would rival their iconic
status within League merchandising. By the end of 'Destination:
Royston Vasey', he seems to have been placed more safely back in the
domain of the comic and the ridiculous, retreating from the world of
Royston Vasey as too freakish even for him. But his first delivery of the
line 'You're my wife now' makes one grateful that the League hadn't yet
ditched their studio audience, as they would from the Christmas Special
onwards. Nervous laughter mixes with audible gasps – *this* is what the
'unresolved tension' between the grotesque, the comic and the uncanny
sounds like.

　　Like any great monster, Lazarou was destined to return, both
times in disguise, first as Santa Claus and then as the effete Keith
Drop. In a review of the Christmas Special in the *Guardian*, Gareth
McLean recalls a childhood nightmare about a 'man with dark skin
and eyes like saucers', claiming that Papa Lazarou's seasonal return as
a demonic Santa realised that nightmare on screen.[116] One of the
inspirations for the character had been Shearsmith's childhood
memory of gypsies coming to his house asking to use the toilet.
Lazarou has been described as a primal figure by the Gents

A shadow over Swanmills: Papa Lazarou

Home invasion: Papa Lazarou   'You're my wife now!'

Childhood trauma and primal Santa: the Christmas Special

themselves,[117] and if Freud's primal father (the original bride-snatcher from *Totem and Taboo*) had had a comedy catchphrase, it would undoubtedly have been 'You're my wife now!' Lazarou possesses his wives by removing their wedding rings, as though they revert to his ownership.[118] In the Christmas Special, Lazarou has become a more malevolent figure than in his original incarnation. Even his absurd insistence on calling all of his victims 'Dave' has become more disturbing: 'Nice to see you again, Dave, *all grown up*'. He emerges progressively from a nightmarish childhood memory, as Bernice remembers her mother being abducted by a faceless Santa.[119] Lazarou's return brings back the whole traumatic memory of an eight-year-old Bernice witnessing this gibbering, screaming figure through the banisters of the stairs. In the Christmas Special's final scene, Lazarou loads the adult Bernice onto his sleigh in a sack and proclaims his marital ownership once more.

Like a number of monsters (most notably, Dracula), Lazarou also became an object of desire. As Gatiss explains:

> I've been told first-hand stories by repressed middle-aged women about
> how much they fancy that character! ... Oh yes, they have fantasies ...
> I imagine somewhere there's some sort of slash fiction about being
> kidnapped by Papa Lazarou. He represents some sort of primal *thing*.
> The dark man at the door who's going to whisk them off![120]

The comments about 'repressed middle-aged women' may not sound
especially generous, but Gatiss isn't wrong about the eroticisation of
Papa (or about the slash fiction). Posters on fan forums sometimes adopt
names like 'Papa's New Wife', suggesting that being abducted by
Lazarou is at the centre of a more diverse set of fantasies than *100
Greatest Scary Moments* might suggest.

Yule Never Leave[121]

The opening sequence of the Christmas Special establishes its seasonal
tone. As a sinister arrangement of 'God Rest Ye, Merry Gentlemen'
plays, the camera descends from the archway of a crypt to a pair of
marble angels, over which the title *The League of Gentlemen* appears. A
moving point-of-view shot, accompanied by heavy breathing, takes us
through a series of despicable pranks: a robin frozen in the snow
snapped off its legs, a snowman's carrot-nose redeployed as his cock, a
piss-spattered snowball hurled at a passing Santa. Each atrocity is
accompanied by a credit for each of the three stars. The nail varnish and
ecclesiastical backdrop yield some incriminating clues, and a reverse
shot confirms that the perpetrator is Reverend Bernice Woodall, a
character who spits bile and bigotry through lipstick-smeared teeth. As
the camera follows her inside, it catches a sign declaring 'God is Dead –
Friedrich Nietzsche', with a white-bearded deity struck in the eye by an
arrow. Merry Christmas.

On Christmas Eve, Bernice receives three visitors, Charlie
Hull, Matthew Parker (a new character, played in flashback by
Shearsmith) and Dr Chinnery. Charlie, like the characters in *Vault of*

Opening titles: Christmas Special

Horror (1973), is haunted by 'the same bloody dream night after night'. Matthew has a terrible memory from his 1970s' youth when 'I knew nothing of the world and all its rottenness.' And Chinnery reveals that his veterinary misfortunes can be traced back to a supernatural Victorian origin. Bernice provides the link between these stories, and a diabolical cigarette lighter with a flame high enough to constitute an

Diabolical Reverend? Charlie and Bernice

offensive weapon seems to place her in a lineage that includes Dr Terror and Peter Cushing's antiques shopkeeper. But the Reverend has a terrible memory of her own of a Christmas Eve when she was eight.

Charlie and Stella have their origins in sketches that were initially variations on a recurring formula, always channelling their marital discord through a third party: a waiter, a baby, Stella's lover or their offscreen daughter Julie. A brief sequence revisits this format, as recriminations fly during the Christmas decorations ritual, with Julie as the (offscreen) go-between, although the punchline reveals that she's at college. In 'Solutions', the first story in the Christmas Special, Charlie has taken up line-dancing in an attempt to find a hobby to share with his wife. Stella is having an affair with Lee, the husband of her best friend, Donna (Liza Tarbuck, given an oily complexion cruelly emphasised by a fish-eye lens.)

In expanding this vision of domestic purgatory, Pemberton and Shearsmith look not so much to the battling couples of music-hall/ seaside postcard comedy, but to perhaps the most atypical episode in an Amicus horror film. 'An Act of Kindness', the second story in *From beyond the Grave*, features Ian Bannen as a lower-middle-class clerk trapped in a soul-destroying job and a home life that consists of unappetising meals and endless arguments with wife Diana Dors. An undistinguished ex-serviceman, Bannen attempts to buy and then steals a medal from Peter Cushing's shop. In doing so, he appears to impress another old soldier, Donald Pleasence, who sells matches and introduces Bannen to his strange but compelling daughter (Angela Pleasence). The tone is darkly comic. Pleasence senior boasts that his daughter 'reads books with jaw cracking words', and she obliges with a demonstration: 'Judicial manners are a matter for prudential judgement.' Blessed with magical powers, she dispatches Dors with a voodoo ritual, but in a twist, also brings about Bannen's demise on their wedding day; father and daughter have been acting on behalf of the couple's son. 'Solutions' retains the voodoo aspect of that story, used by Stella to humiliate Charlie during the line-dancing competition that means so much to him. Like 'An Act of Kindness', the story is an essay in emasculation, with women either uncanny or malicious (or both), but sides much more with its put-upon male character. Charlie and Stella might share a similar sense of disappointment, but she is undoubtedly cast as being less sympathetic. The line-dancing is supposed to bring them closer, but

91

Domestic hell: Charlie and Stella

Royston Vasey's matriarchal cabal

Stella rejects this reconciliatory gesture and seems especially galled that Charlie should be good at something. The voodoo spell is cast by a kind of matriarchal cabal, cowls and *Eyes Wide Shut* masks offering a thin disguise for recognisable Vasey women: Pauline, Judee, Iris, Vinnie and Reenie, even the incomprehensible Pam Doove. As the voodoo doll of Charlie catches fire, to much consternation, the Vasey coven also recalls the comic bra-burning feminists of *Carry on Girls* (1973). Charlie is thoroughly humiliated, slow-handclapped and soaked in beer, but the full Amicus-style punishment is reserved for Stella. As she gloats with Lee, his throat is cut via another voodoo ritual and Donna is revealed as cuckolded avenger. An overhead shot finds Stella surrounded by police, clutching an incriminating razor over her lover's blood-soaked body.

Don't Let the Bugger Bite You: 'The Vampire of Duisburg'

Story two poses the question: is the self-proclaimed 'Queen of Duisburg' actually 'The Vampire of Duisburg'? The guess-the-vampire story again recalls Amicus. In 'Vampire' (*Dr Terror's House of Horrors*) and

'Midnight Mess' (*Vault of Horror*), vampires must be detected within
the quotidian world, with plot twists the order of the day. 'The Vampire
of Duisburg' was originally the opening tale, but shifted to the middle
slot at the suggestion of producer Jemma Rodgers. It would certainly
make an attention-grabbing opening turn; of the three stories, it offers
the most sustained use of outright horror. Its ultimate positioning,
however, adds to the Christmas Special's cumulative build as well as its
progressive move backwards in time (1975 and 1895). As the older
Matthew (Andrew Melville) begins his tale, a Christmas decoration in
the shape of a bespectacled choirboy cuts to a real choirboy, a caption
'Duisburg 1975', followed by another cut to a bat-like Lipp conducting
his 'queerboys'. For the first time, *The League of Gentlemen* moves to a
different temporal and geographic location, but Duisburg proves to be
an uncanny mirror image of Vasey, flashing headlights catching the sign
outside Herr Lipp's house that reads 'Schwannmuhle-weg' (Swanmill
Way).[122] Matthew is an orphan of uncertain age; 'How old is the boy?'
was Jon Plowman's concerned question, but Shearsmith's casting
alleviates the problem. He arrives in Duisburg to join the choir of
orphans presided over by Herr Lipp and his wife ('but not in fuck'),

93

Back in time: Duisburg 1975

Lotte. The innuendo has lost none of its lustre. 'O Come in My Faceful' is Lipp's idea of a carol, while he tells Matthew that 'some of the older (boys) can be quite a mouthful'. To the already popular catchphrase 'alles klar' – the postmodern 'I'm free!' if you will – he adds an even better one, 'Sleep tight – don't let the bugger bite you!'

'Vampire' capitalises on the narrative 'bubble' within which the Christmas Special takes place. This isn't *quite* the same Lipp who will arrive in Vasey twenty-five years later. The Lipp of series two is a Rohypnol-wielding paedophile, but while Matthew is implicitly (perhaps narrowly) under age, he is conspicuously older than the other choirboys. Nevertheless, incriminating evidence mounts, playing on a longstanding correlation between vampirism and queer sexuality. When Matthew announces that 'I know what you are!', they aren't entirely singing from the same carol sheet. Lipp casts a *Nosferatu* shadow, and quotes Klaus Kinski's incarnation of the character, 'The absence of love is the most abject pain.' The riskiest scene shows him playing party games with his boys, lederhosened *Kinder* riding on his back. As

Herr Lipp as Nosferatu

Herr Lipp taking a mouthful

Matthew watches through a semi-open door, Lipp drinks some
unknown red concoction that dribbles obscenely down his chin.

It isn't just Herr Lipp who can't keep his eyes off Matthew's
groin; the camera can't either. One scene casts Lipp as Norman Bates to
Matthew's Marion Crane. Lipp presses his eye to a concealed spyhole as
the boy strips to tight 70s' underpants and scratches his crotch. This
spectacle is relayed via Lipp's literal point of view, but during Matthew's
later nightmare, the camera remains at crotch level as he makes his way
across the room. In other words, we are invited into this queer gaze,
seeing him exactly as Lipp does. Even more than Benjamin in the first
two series, Matthew is cast as gothic heroine both investigating and
trapped within the terrible house, rendered even more threatening by
low camera angles and shadowed ceilings.[123] Like Benjamin, Matthew is
also adopted as a surrogate child, his bedroom full of sinister toys, a
ludicrously small chair that he can't extricate himself from, and the
cramped wooden cot that he sleeps in. This links the room to Lotte, a
frustrated maternal vampire with nipples like nuclear missiles and Max

Schreck fangs. 'You could never give me boys, Wolf, so I had to provide my own', she cries, as the vamped-up boys descend on their 'queermaster'. But Matthew will have two unforgettable encounters with Herr Lipp in that room. The first is a genuinely frightening nightmare sequence in which Matthew is woken by a billowing, wind-buffeted curtain and a madly rocking wooden horse. Lipp's ghostly voice alerts him to a mysterious key in his hand, and Matthew discovers his own corpse, blue-skinned, eyes and mouth sewn shut, in the wardrobe. He looks up to see Lipp pinned insect-like to the ceiling, fanged and yellow-eyed. Textbook gothic TV, it's a sequence that underlines just how much Steve Bendelack brings to *The League of Gentlemen*. [124] The second sequence is a reworking of Lipp's attempted seduction of 'my very own Justin' in series two, but lighter on the menace and higher on the pathos. On Christmas Eve, he appears drunk and giggly in Matthew's bedroom with his present, a bottle of Brut, flirtatiously allows his dressing gown to fall open, accidentally sits on a crucifix fashioned from a toothbrush, and mistakes the smell of

96

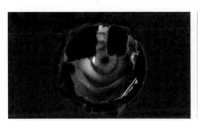

Herr Lipp admiring Matthew's attributes

Maternal vampire: Lotte Lipp

Matthew's nightmare

Homophobia and vampire panic:
Lipp and Matthew on Christmas Eve

Lipp sucked off by his 'queerboys'

protective garlic tablets for flatulence. 'I hope you understand that sometimes the inside of something can be beautiful even if the package isn't ... well, *isn't*', he implores the boy. In a sublimely framed shot, both funny and touching, Lipp places the aftershave tenderly on the pillow as Matthew, in the background, clutches a toy rabbit in front of his crotch, transfixed by a mixture of homophobia and vampire panic. 'Leave me alone!' cries the boy, and Lipp's response confirms that this is a less predatory incarnation of the character: 'I will try.' Lipp will sacrifice himself to save Matthew when Lotte's children turn on them in the story's climax.

Victorian Vasey (or 'The Monkey's Bollocks'): 'The Curse of Karrit Poor'

If 'Solutions' and 'The Vampire of Duisburg' partly derive from Amicus-style tales, 'The Curse of Karrit Poor' evokes more televisual tales of terror, in particular, the BBC's adaptations of M. R. James. Although the most acclaimed James adaptation, Jonathan Miller's *Whistle and I'll Come to You* (BBC, 1968), was made for the arts programme *Omnibus*, the BBC's 'Ghost Story for Christmas' became a particular institution between 1971 and 1978, with producer Lawrence Gordon Clark overseeing fondly remembered adaptations of James (five in all), before moving on to Dickens's *The Signalman* (1975) and ending with two less celebrated original stories. Christmas 1972 offered a veritable gothic feast, with James's *A Warning to the Curious*, Nigel Kneale's chilling *The Stone Tape* and episodes of the anthology series *Dead of Night* broadcast on the BBC over the season. During the same Christmas period as the League's Special, the BBC returned to M. R. James with *Christopher Lee's Ghost Stories for Christmas*, with Lee as James telling his stories to students at King's College. These programmes exemplify the 'gentlemanly restraint' of the BBC ghost story, an aesthetic of 'showing less, suggesting more', although Helen Wheatley reminds us that they could conjure up some disturbing imagery for their climaxes.[125] The spectre haunting Denholm Elliott in *The Signalman* is what the Spirit of Dark and Lonely Water might have looked like if he had lifted his cowl. Jeremy Dyson is an eloquent spokesperson for the tradition of 'gentlemanly restraint' (even if one would need to look hard to find that quality in the League) and Mark Gatiss's fondness for historical pastiche has already been cited. 'Karrit Poor', along with the framing story, was their collaborative contribution to the Christmas Special.

'The Curse of Karrit Poor' has some comic precursors too. Some of Dave Allen's most enduring stories and sketches take their inspiration from the horror genre. Gatiss has fond memories of the moments when the lights would dim for the comedian's creepier tales; 'As a child I remember he used to tell those spooky stories and they were genuinely frightening. And then he'd pull the rug out at the last minute and make you laugh, but he was a master, a master storyteller.' In addition to his oral tales, atmospheric sketches shot on film provided affectionate parodies of classic gothic horror cinema. It should come as no surprise that Allen was first choice for the part of Mr Purblind. Even more pertinent, though, is 'The Curse of the Claw', an episode of Michael Palin and Terry Jones's *Ripping Yarns*. Both stories allude to W. W. Jacobs's *The Monkey's Paw* (1902) and, more generally, the kind of 'imperial Gothic' in which an artefact from the East brings misfortune to whoever takes possession of it.[126] The exact nature of the curse in *The Monkey's Paw*, one that operates through the granting of wishes, is deployed more explicitly through the Dentons' Colombian Natterjack Toad (2.1), the stroking of which brings a bedraggled Benjamin 'home' much like the dead son in Jacobs's story. In 'The Curse of the Claw', the artefact in question is the claw of the Burmese vulture. The framing story is set in 1926, but then takes us back to the Victorian era, with lots of jokes about the period's supposed prudishness. The effect of the curse is to snatch the hero (Palin) from the modern world and to regress him to his Victorian childhood, doomed to live through the era again.

In 'Karrit Poor', the curse is used to establish a supernatural origin for the misfortunes of Mr Chinnery, the hapless vet who

inadvertently (and gorily) terminates the life of every pet brought into his
care. We first encounter his great grandfather as an esteemed London
veterinary surgeon in 1895, a 'modern St Francis', completing a
successful operation on a rabbit, watched by a rapt audience (including
Jeremy Dyson) and the rabbit's owner, Mrs Trevithick. Chinnery is
summoned by Dr Majolica, a saturnine figure whose phrase 'sit down as
usual' anticipates series three's Dr Carlton, and dispatched to Royston
Vasey, where he will join the practice of Purblind, Boothby and Canker.
Like any Gothic house worth its salt, the home of Singleton Boothby is
filled with secrets and forbidden rooms ('All my doors are open to you,
Chinnery, except for the ones that are closed.') The mystery pertains to
Purblind, the senior partner, confined to his room and not to be
disturbed. Woken by cries in the night, Chinnery finds his way by
candlelight to Purblind's room, stopping only to find a cowled figure in a
rocking chair with a suspiciously Lazarou-like voice. Bedridden, Purblind
amuses himself with a magic lantern show, depicting Chinnery's candlelit
search with preternatural foresight. Purblind uses the lantern show to tell
the tale of his curse. It isn't the monkey's paw, but the monkey's bollocks
that have bestowed the malady in question. Purblind was chief vet to the

London 1895: a modern St Francis

Jeremy Dyson in the audience

Chinnery is expected

Magic lantern show:
Topov the 'cheeky monkey'

Colonial gothic:
the Maharajah's revenge

Maharajah of Karrit Poor in India, with particular responsibility for the 101
care of the 'cheeky monkey' Topov,[127] whose amorous activities trapped
his member in an elephant. Topov is cruelly and fatally castrated by the
confusion of verucca acid with Vaseline, and the Maharajah's vengeance
follows on. Tricked into touching Topov's parts, Chinnery steps into the
web that has been spun for him and inherits a hex that will pass through
the family line for generations.

By deepening story continuity and providing a glimpse of a
Victorian Vasey populated by Dickensian counterparts to some of the
series' most popular characters – 'Give me that quill back!' shouts
Victorian Pauline to a Tiny Tim-like Mickey, while a familiar transsexual
hansom cab driver complains of a bloodsoaked bustle 'like the frigging
Crimea' – 'Karrit Poor' presented the most lavish version to date of the
League's 'completely furnished world'. The notion of furnishing points to
another quality that has endeared the story to fans: the high-gothic
production values, hansom cabs, operating theatres, magic lantern
shows and steam engines. This Victoriaphilia, a retro-aesthetic of

Victoriaphilia: Chinnery arrives in Royston Vasey

morbidity and sensation, is a particular characteristic of Gatiss (admittedly even more obsessed with the Edwardian era); 'I have been in love with the morbid, ebony-black grotesqueness of the nineteenth century since I was knee-high to a funeral mute.'[128] His literally Dickensian *Doctor Who* story 'The Unquiet Dead' (BBC1, 2005) typifies Victoriaphilia: undertakers, snow (alongside fog, the default climatic coordinate for the genre), reanimated corpses, gratuitous use of the word 'Phantasmagoria'.

Appropriately for a BBC Christmas Ghost Story, 'The Curse of Karrit Poor' manages (narrowly) the conceit of being an adaptation. It originated as a short story by Gatiss in the spin-off book *A Local Book for Local People*, 'a story so fantastic that it might seem to have sprung from the ravings of some brain-fevered Eastern mystic. Or a twat.'[129] The framing story is Edwardian:

As I write, the new century is scarcely begun. It is the age of invention, of the electric light, the motor car and the gentlemen's shoe and sock. The old queen is dead. It seems impertinent, of course, to refer to him as such, but Dr Timothy Majolica was always 'the old queen' to us in our student days.

As much a pastiche of gentlemen's adventure stories as the English ghost
story, 'Karrit Poor' now seems like a partial dry run for Gatiss's novels
about bisexual spy Lucifer Box, even sharing a character called Jackpot.
Just as *The Vesuvius Club* queers the (already homosocial) world of
gentlemen's fiction ('For the well-bred gentleman there was surely only
one recourse. I fucked him'),[130] so too does the original 'Karrit Poor', with
a rather different Majolica giving Greek lessons to boys from the Poor
School. As Chinnery travels to Vasey by train, the town receives its most
gothic treatment, 'a bleak landscape of skeletal trees and frozen
waterways', where the TV version can't resist a saucy parody of *The
Railway Children* (1970). On a DVD extra, Gatiss, in Edwardian
costume, stroking a stuffed cat, narrates the story to camera as a
mocked-up episode of *Jackanory* (BBC, 1965–96), a nod to oral ghost
storytelling that evokes Dave Allen as much as M. R. James. Dyson helped
flesh out the story for its TV incarnation. Gatiss's original story ends with
the bestowing of the curse, but the TV version adds an apocalyptic
denouement that depicts the first gruesome manifestation of Chinnery's
curse. Attempting a surgical tap to the skull of Mrs Trevithick's rabbit, he
unwittingly sets in motion a trail of carnage that spreads from surgery to
waiting room and out into the street (and a passing circus); cats, parrots,
tigers and elephants perish horribly and Chinnery is left clutching the
severed head of a zebra, patting it ineffectually. The scale of the slaughter
notwithstanding, the climax also brings us back to the repetitions of
sketch comedy that the Christmas Special otherwise leaves behind; we
have seen this happen to the contemporary Chinnery many times. 'Karrit
Poor' is the richest, arguably the most satisfying of the three stories, but it
is also the least disturbing, containing nothing of the marital bleakness of
'Solutions' or the nightmarish dream sequence of 'The Vampire of
Duisburg'. Nevertheless, the Christmas Special could not be accused of
ending on a cosy note. As Bernice is about to undergo a Scrooge-like
conversion, she finds she has one last seasonal visitor who remembers her
from when she was eight. The menace lingers into the dying moments of
the programme; behind the director and producer credits, a single
white-rimmed eye stares malevolently out of the darkness.

103

The Railway Children ...

... but not as we remember it

'Oh dear, oh dear':
Chinnery and zebra head

The menace lingers: the final shot

104

The League's Christmas Special would not only consummate their love affair with the gothic and the uncanny, but mark a new ambition in their storytelling. Many regard it as their best work, and you won't find any opposition to that view here. Dyson calls it 'the apotheosis of everything that had gone before'.

> The engine was running so well by then that everybody knew what they were doing. We had an inner confidence about what had worked, and what we wanted to do, and so it was one of those rare joyous experiences where no effort was required. It was a joyful thing to do, and I'm sure that's one of the reasons why it looks the way it does.

It would be almost two years before the League produced new material about Royston Vasey, but their third series would be both their most ambitious and their most contentious.

5 Follow the Red Bag

This is the lost series of *The League of Gentlemen*.

Mark Gatiss, series three DVD commentary

While 'backlash' is too strong a word for series three's critical
reception, there nevertheless clings to it a sense of being undervalued.
BBC2 has never repeated it; it finally came 'home' on BBC4 in 2006.
The notion of the 'difficult' third series again links the League to
Monty Python, whose third outing is sometimes presented as troubled.
John Cleese has always maintained that repetition had set in, and
Roger Wilmut discerns 'a tendency for some of the material to become
weird rather than funny',[131] an accusation that the League are
probably familiar with. Cleese adhered to two series of *Fawlty Towers*
and, more recently, Ricky Gervais has maintained two as the magic
number with both *The Office* and *Extras* (BBC2, 2005–6).[132]
The League were aware of the series three stigma and saw it as a
challenge. 'There's that thing that third series are never that good',
says Dyson. '(We thought), "Oh, we'll try and make a good one – we'll
show them."' A video diary formed part of BBC Choice's *The Making
of Series Three*, with more of it featured on the DVD, and reinforces
the impression that this was a tough series to write. However, Dyson
offers the interesting theory that recording the creative process for
DVD posterity didn't so much capture extended bouts of writer's
block as help create them:

I mean, you'd turn the fucking camera on every time you sat down to write, and me and Mark couldn't do anything until the tape had run out, so anything that's on that camera is just completely artificial because the work didn't begin until the tape had run out. I seriously think – and I don't know if the others know I think this – that that third series would be better if we hadn't agreed to have done that.[133]

Gatiss, on the other hand, feels that the series was less collaborative than previous ones. Episode 3.1 was written solely by Pemberton and Shearsmith, and 3.2 by Dyson and Gatiss.

The cooler response to the third series of *The League of Gentlemen* isn't immediately apparent if one takes its reviews in isolation. There had always been dissenting voices among the chorus of praise that greeted series one and two. Watching the start of the second series, for example, Nick Patton Walsh not only 'missed the joke' of Papa Lazarou, but judged the 'recent rise in surreal humour' as symptomatic of a national malaise: 'We are no longer comfortable laughing at our sorry Americanized selves. Instead we choose to laugh at situations and sentences that are merely nonsensical as opposed to satirical – moronic as opposed to ironic.'[134]

Reviewing series three's first episode, Gerard O'Donovan confessed to never having found the series 'very funny or even engaging, beyond being shocked by its brute originality when it first appeared in 1999', but was intrigued, if not exactly entertained, by the gender-bending aspects of the episode.[135] A vituperative review in the *Daily Mail* was read out by the Gents in *The Making of Series Three* and reproduced defiantly in *Scripts and That*. On the other hand, Gareth McLean's opinion that series three was 'bolder, funnier and more daring than ever' was far from a lone voice.[136] But when *Radio Times*' Alison Graham opined that the League had been critically 'overshadowed' by the second series of *The Office*, she hit the nail on the head.[137] Gervais's sitcom had become the most celebrated British sitcom since *The Royle Family* and its ratings were about to blossom, while the League's had declined slightly. The League featured in *Radio Times*' 'Today's Choices'

throughout series three (Graham had been an ardent supporter since
series one), but it was *The Office* that grabbed the front cover on its
return. 'When something else comes along that's the new golden boy',
says Dyson, looking back, 'it's a bit disconcerting. It knocks your
confidence a bit.'

If the critical honeymoon had cooled only slightly (and
comparatively), there was a more tangible shift in the popular reception
of series three. Amazon.co.uk's customer reviews provide a small, but
revealing, sample of this response. For series one and two and the
Christmas Special, the response is almost unanimously positive, with 5/5
stars being the most common rating, no 2s or 3s and a token 1 star from
someone who doesn't 'get' the show; 'gross, perverted to the point of
depravity and totally unfunny' is the sort of bad press easily converted
into good.[138] The response to series three is striking. For one thing, there
are more than twice as many reviews, suggesting that it was more
contentious. More than half give the series 5/5, but there is more of a
spread through the other ratings, and a number of negative reviews.
The following is representative of some recurring complaints:

107

> totally uninspired new characters, the absence of many beloved old
> characters ... situations which were either sick (like the stubbing out of
> cigarettes on someone's arm), completely unfunny (see the dog cinema or
> the 'do you want your breasts pinched?' man) or sick and unfunny (Charlie's
> stint in the massage parlour). The music was changed horribly too, and the
> laugh track was dropped to the detriment of the programme, although I
> think that was because if it had been put in there would have been precious
> little laughter on it.[139]

If 'bad' (outraged) reviews can sometimes be converted into 'good' ones,
the reverse can occasionally happen, too: 'It's not meant to be funny!'
insists one defensive reviewer.[140]

The League themselves seem ambivalent about the series,
proud of individual elements but uncertain about its overall shape and
tone. For Dyson, it's a 'curate's egg':

that isn't to disrespect the work we did on it – I mean, it's got some fantastic stuff in it. I think: What would it be if we'd done it this way, if we'd sliced the cake differently so that it was more like the first two series but with those narrative elements? So rather than us telling whole stories, with each character in each week, what would it be like if you'd had bits of each story each week? Steve (Pemberton) observed at the time, if you don't like a character in that week, you're stuck with them, whereas one of the joys of the form is that if you don't like a character it doesn't matter because you only have to stick with them for a couple of minutes and the one that you do like will come on again – (in series three) you're asking a different thing of the audience.

Gatiss feels similarly. 'Although I'm very proud of that series, we didn't jump the shark but we certainly got one foot on the water ski in terms of what the public were expecting versus what we wanted to do.' This feeling seems inseparable from the series' reception:

It's forever tinged with the fact that it wasn't repeated, we didn't get much of a sense of a thrill from the BBC, and the one thing you cannot hide from (is someone saying) 'I love your show. I didn't like the last (series), mind – it was very weak.' It just gets you in the guts, and we got that because it was different, and I think that inevitably tinges your mindset.

I favour the word 'flawed' over curates' eggs or water skis. These are probably fine distinctions, even taking into account the distance between creator and viewer. Series three is more ambitious even than the Christmas Special, which had generic templates to fall back on in developing longer narratives. In my view, its first three episodes stand among the League's best TV work. Episode 4 isn't far behind, but while episode 5 is interesting, I do have some sympathy with viewers who find Charlie's climactic beating unnecessarily cruel and depressing.[141] Only the final episode justifies some of the more negative reactions. Papa Lazarou remains fascinating, even if his stint as Keith Drop helps disguise the fact that his possibilities as a returning Big Bad are limited.

But sequences dealing with a dog-themed cinema don't seem to catch fire, and Dean Tavalouris strikes me as a misjudged character.

The format changes are worth detailing. There is the funkier arrangement of the theme tune, described by Joby Talbot as 'the Stevie Wonder version'.[142] For the second time, the studio audience is absent, a decision that could be viewed as either risky, given an even grimmer tone, or providing the freedom for a more narrative-based, less gag-filled, approach. At the time of the first series in 1999, the League told interviewers that they added a laugh track (reluctantly) because they weren't sure the audience would immediately recognise that it was a comedy. Once seen as a signifier of 'liveness', the use of recorded laughter in TV comedy was intended to be 'contagious', as well as binding the fragmented TV audience into a unified 'presence'.[143] Studio audiences were supposedly more authentic than canned laughter, but this was not always the case in practice; they could be nervous or laugh too loud or too long.[144] Brett Mills sees the decline of recorded laughter as the most significant development for TV comedy since the three-camera set-up,[145] and its absence has become a sign of 'quality', of crediting the audience with the intelligence to judge what is funny.[146] On the other hand, when *Little Britain* retained its studio audience over three series and a pair of Christmas Specials, it clearly signalled its populist credentials, one of the ways in which, in spite of some similarities to *The League of Gentlemen*, it saw itself as a less exclusive series. Perhaps the most telling change of all is staged in the pre-credits sequence of 3.1, a veritable statement of intent. Initially, all seems present and correct, if slightly the worse for wear: the Vasey sign, Babs and her cab bringing flowers to David's 'grave', the charred husk of the Local Shop. Two pairs of hands burst from the rubble, one clutching a snow globe. Royston Vasey's two most popular inhabitants rise from their would-be tombs ... only to be turned into intercity roadkill by the train that they had planned on taking to London.

Each episode of series three focuses mainly on a single character or group of characters. 'The Lesbian and the Monkey' (3.1) follows Pauline from prison to the outside world, where she is drawn

109

Kill your icons: Tubbs and Edward about to be intercity roadkill

into an unholy alliance with her nemesis, Ross. In 'The One Armed Man Is King' (3.2), joke-shop owner Lance has a transplant to replace his missing arm. 'Turn Again, Geoff Tipps' (3.3) follows the would-be jester to London in pursuit of a stand-up career, while 'The Medusa Touch' (3.4) tracks the consequences of one of Alvin and Sunny's swinging parties. In 'Beauty and the Beast (or Come into My Parlour)' (3.5), Charlie works for Judee at the Spit'n'Polish beauty salon, offering massages that escalate into 'extras' and lead to an unexpected unrequited love. 'How the Elephant Got Its Trunk' (3.6) is less clearly focused on one character, but features the return of the charity-shop workers and Papa Lazarou.

Pauline, Geoff and Charlie are obvious candidates for these extended narratives, Lance and Alvin perhaps less so. Lance might seem a more sketch-bound character, selling mean-spirited 'tricks' reminiscent of Terry Jones's chocolate manufacturer filling confectionary with crunchy frogs or larks' vomit in *Monty Python*. The episode opens with a reminder of his sketchier origins, as he tries to sell inappropriate items to a young boy ('Stag night, is it?') and his grandmother. But Lance's story plays like the missing fourth episode of the Christmas Special, and is none the worse for it. The series is unified not so much by an 'arc' as an event that ties the climaxes of each episode together. Pauline is distracted by a red plastic bag blowing, *American Beauty* fashion, in the wind and almost struck by a white van (3.1). The episode ends on a cliffhanger, a POV shot representing the van speeding towards her. She is rescued by Lance, who, prompted by the ghostly former owner of his arm, sacrifices himself to save her (3.2). The van, stolen from Legz Akimbo, is driven by Geoff, escaping from London after unwittingly aiding a terrorist attack (3.3). At the Windermere Hotel, a 'swinging' party ends in tragedy when an exercise in erotic asphyxiation backfires. One of the casualties is Sunny, and Alvin buries the bodies in the garden. Unbeknown to him, Sunny has invited makeover maestro Laurence Llewelyn Bowen to oversee a new patio, and the flamboyant TV presenter perishes when the white van bursts through the wall (3.4). On his way to the Windermere, Charlie is struck by rubble from the damaged wall, and carried off by Keith Drop (3.5). Keith is actually Papa Lazarou, who takes Charlie to the Pandemonium Carnival, placing him, bizarrely, inside an elephant with Brian and Bernice (her Christmas fate finally revealed) (3.6).[147]

The red bag appears in all six episodes as a marker of temporal simultaneity, blowing out of the window of the charity shop (its first chronological appearance) and subsequently leading Vinnie to her death when she loses control of her vehicle (3.6) or floating past Charlie as he gazes, besotted, at Tony (3.5). There are other such continuities. The grandmother who buys a hideously detailed dildo from Lance (3.2) takes it to the Steele's party, where it squirts artificial cum in Alvin's face (3.4). There is a degree of thematic unity, too. With the exception of Geoff, the central characters undergo shifts in their sexual identities. Pauline, fresh from flicking through 'librarians' in the 'Clitclink', agrees to marry Mickey, but this turn to heterosexuality happens under decidedly queer circumstances. At Barbara's gender-bending party, they are both in drag, *Killing of Sister George*-style, Pauline as Beryl Reid/Oliver Hardy, Mickey as Susannah York. In his otherwise hostile review, Gerard O'Donovan was taken by 'the extraordinary sight of a

111

Joined-up endings: Pauline and the red bag

The Legz Akimbo van after the accident

Keith Drop carries off Charlie

The red bag: Vinnie led to her doom

Charlie watching Tony

113

The Killing of Sister Pauline: the gender-bending party

Changing sexual identities: Lance's feminine arm

Film beige: Judith and Alvin

Charlie declares his love for Tony

man playing a man dressed as a woman attempting to make passionate love to a man playing a woman dressed as a man.'[148] Lance is feminised by his new arm and, in an inverted 'possession' narrative, by the civilising influence of its former owner, a nun. Pouring himself a beer, he finds that he has put a cocktail umbrella in it, and attempts to re-masculinise himself by pumping iron, getting a tattoo and gluing hair on the rogue limb. Alvin pursues a chaste version of a film noir (film beige?) affair with drab Judith, who represents an illicit alternative to Sunny's sexual regime ('You're staying here to explore your sexuality with the rest of us!') Charlie finds himself attracted to his rival for Stella, Tony, donning a blond wig and eyeliner. Keith Drop is the camp alter ego of Lazarou, whose 'wives' are clearly less gender-specific than they might once have seemed. What price gender difference when everyone is called 'Dave'?

'The Lesbian and the Monkey', 'The Medusa Touch' and 'Come into My Parlour' deal with contrasting sexual triangles: Pauline/Mickey/Ross, Alvin/Sunny/Judith and Charlie/Stella/Tony. 'The Lesbian and the Monkey' is Ross's appellation for Pauline and Mickey when he discovers that they have become engaged. Sporting a new, shorter hairstyle that we're clearly meant to read as 'prison dyke', Pauline is first seen 'going for the pink' in the women's prison she dominates, doling out her vibrator the Exocet and trading favours for her beloved pens. Ross has become unequivocally villainous, using Pauline as a mole to convict Mickey for benefit fraud, just stopping himself before using the words 'dole scum'. 'Why are you doing this, Ross?' she asks tearfully after a bout of aggressive, joyless impulse sex and his threat to tell Mickey. 'Because you made me hate my job', he replies. This dangerous mutual attraction arrives from nowhere, and doesn't necessarily make much psychological sense, but it keeps the Pauline–Ross dynamic on an unpredictable path.

Sunny, described in the script as 'well preserved and dangerously glamorous',[149] is one of the few prominent female characters not played in drag, the casting of actress Christine Furness signalling that her robust, middle-aged glamour is to be taken at face

115

Pauline 'going for the pink'

116

Dangerous Liaisons: Ross and Pauline

value. The joke is the discrepancy between Sunny's aggressive 'swinging' voyage and Alvin's preference for Alistair MacLean and panto routines that lose whatever humour they held in the telling ('he fires the bloomin' arrow and he's shot, of course!') Like Basil Fawlty before him, Alvin was based on the owner of a real hotel where Dyson and Gatiss stayed. The real 'Alvin' had a glamorous wife, prompting some speculation about their secret life. Who is most perverse here, the series seems to ask, the middle-aged woman who still expects sex to be dangerous and exciting or the man who is more turned on by *Watercolour Challenge* (Channel 4, 1998–2000)? 'We just thought, "There's something going on here"', says Gatiss. 'What really amused us was the idea he'd much rather read *Where Eagles Dare* and have a quiet night in than have sex all night.' The title sequence of 3.4 plays on their contrasting agendas: as he puts on his surgical collar,[150] she puts on a choker; he reads a Seed Catalogue, she peruses a magazine entitled *Drowning in Jizz*; each trims their respective 'bush' (one horticultural, one pubic). Alvin is in love with dowdy Judith, whose eyebrows look not so much painted as carved with a Stanley knife. She proves to be as 'dangerous' as Sunny, prompting Alvin to bury the sexplorers in the garden after they succumb to the asphyxiating 'Medusa', a fantastical device operated by the Pan-like roué 'Daddy'. Papa Lazarou, Pop, Daddy – do we detect a pattern

117

Contrasting desires –
Alvin's 'Seed Catalogue'

Sunny 'drowning in jizz'

Alvin and Sunny trim their 'bushes'

developing here? Tanya Krzywinska characterises the 'Demon Daddy' in the horror genre as primal and medieval, the 'supreme corruptor'.[151] This figure, sexually threatening and amoral, grotesque in Michael Steig's sense of the word, keeps haunting *The League of Gentlemen*.

Charlie and Stella had always operated by way of a triangle, the third party through whom they channelled their hatred of one another. *On the Town* hints that this 'hatred' is a form of love; when they consider separating, it's abuse that brings them back together. The TV series, however, is less forgiving. According to René Girard, in European literature dealing with romantic triangles, the homoerotic bonds between male rivals are stronger and more intense than those between either rival and their female prize.[152] This being comedy (very *knowing* comedy), we need to qualify this slightly; in Charlie and Tony's case, repressed homosexual desire only goes one way. As customers lie blindfolded, Charlie performs massage (a skill acquired in the homosocial environment of the merchant navy) to mainly male clients. As his repertoire extends, so too does his reputation, and Judee starts wondering why the towels are stiff. Tony had first surfaced on screen in series two, revealed as Stella's lover during a game of Trivial Pursuit (2.6). An earlier appearance as daughter Julie's boyfriend was cut from series one; if it hadn't been, then he would have effectively captivated the entire Hull family. Initially appalled by Tony's arrival at the salon, Charlie's head is turned by what he finds under the towel. In fact, his head is more than turned, judging by a later gag about tickly moustaches. Macho working-class Charlie can neither comprehend nor fully articulate these new feelings; when he tells Tony he loves him, he insists it's 'not in a queer way'. Dominant heterosexual culture, Eve Kosofsky Sedgwick argues, insists on a break in the continuum between the homosocial (male bonding) and the homosexual, but Charlie has lost his bearings on that continuum.[153] Little wonder that he ends up as one of Papa Lazarou's wives, carried off by 'Keith' after the accident.

'Turn Again, Geoff Tipps' stands apart from the sexual dramas that otherwise seem to bind series three. Instead, our eponymous hero negotiates both the north–south divide and the world of professional

Charlie acquires a new skill

comedy. Mike arrives with bad news, and there's a reminder that Geoff is a less than ideal employee:

> MIKE: You know, don't you, that head office has decided to scale down the injection mouldings side and put more resources into absorbents?
> GEOFF: (nodding sagely) I know there's a head office.

Geoff bounces back with a journey to London to pursue his comic aspirations. In the big smoke, there's much play on the northerner 'abroad', negotiating ticket machines and the Tube, but by often focusing on trendy Camden, the episode offers an unflattering picture of London that largely concurs with Geoff's view of 'clever London people'. Most appalling of all is fag hag Tish, a cruelly but not inaccurately observed character dating back to the live shows. 'I love gay guys', she tells Legz Akimbo's Phil, forlorn after splitting from his boyfriend, 'You're so vulnerable and yet not at all threatening.'

The high point of the episode is Geoff's stand-up act, which departs from borrowed stories like 'Mau Mau' to attempt something observational based on regional differences – 'It's that divide.

Northerner abroad – Geoff and 'the Tubes'

120

Clever London people – Tish and Phil in Camden

Northerners generally are more friendly than you lot.' After a promising start, he becomes too Local. The trendy crowd don't recognise the reference points or see what's odd about Tube travel etiquette, and Vasey men driving Robin Reliants don't cross the comedy divide. He starts to flounder ('What else? I'm sweating!') and polite laughter dries up into hostile silence. The TV producer he can't take his eyes off starts sending a text message. Geoff responds with characteristic good grace:

> GEOFF: So why do you bother? Why do you bother coming out if you're not gonna laugh? ... . 'Cos it's easy this, isn't it? Any of you could do this better than me, I'm just crap.
> HECKLER [Jeremy Dyson]: Get off then!
> GEOFF: Don't worry, I will! (cheer from another heckler) Oh, fuck off!

This is what critics a few years earlier had been calling 'the comedy of cringe'. As the lights go off, it looks as though he might actually have to be dragged off stage; 'Oh yeah, yeah, turn the lights off!' he continues in splenetic overdrive. In a dream, the same act is a triumph at a big London theatre, with eager fans wearing T-shirts with his catchphrase on ('Tubes'). Pleasingly, the series finale offers him some compensation; in hospital after the crash, he gets a much better response

Robin Reliants and their relation to the unconscious – Geoff on stage

King of Comedy: Geoff's dream of success

to his Robin Reliant material from the medical staff (and Mike) who surround his bed.

Series three doesn't represent a complete break from the sketch format: each episode is filled out by less developed material, mainly featuring new characters. Lance's episode, for example, also includes debt collectors Barry and Glenn Baggs, and a Gatiss monologue that is the companion to 'Stumphole Cavern', but more minimally (and satisfyingly) realised on screen. Like Mick McNamara, the mortician Owen Fallowfield suggests the influence of Bennett's *Talking Heads*; Gatiss, like Dyson, admired 'the incredible spareness of the story-telling and yet a world of suggestion and beautiful things'. In Bennett's darker, later monologues, the humour is more low key as we encounter a child-molester or the wife of a serial killer. 'Playing Sandwiches' (BBC2, 1998), starring David Haig as a park keeper who can't keep away from children, is not overtly comic apart from a line attributed to his wife: 'If you made a decision never to buy another liquorice allsort, it would be a step in the right direction.' Owen, we gradually learn, is a necrophile, which in the realm of 'sick' humour, makes him a 'safer' character than a paedophile, grist to the 'dark comedy' mill; 'I said, "I'm paid to plug their cavities." He said, 'Not all of them, sunshine "'

What transforms the material into something more than a ticking off of comedy's taboos is not only Gatiss's commanding performance, captured in long takes during which he progressively meets 'our' gaze, but the sense that, if Owen is less immediately tragic than Mick, he has been transformed or brought into focus by a very real darkness.

> When you've been stood on a Christmas morning with some poor woman
> screaming and screaming 'cos her kiddy's gone under the wheels of a
> Vauxhall Astra, all the mystery goes out of it somehow. *No* – no God.

The comic is confined to the banality of detail – not any car, a Vauxhall Astra – but having glimpsed the abyss, Owen emerges as a moral vacuum. 'Is it wrong?' he asks. 'I don't know. You know what they say – the only things you regret are the things you don't do.' A creepy grin returns us to the comic monster as the police lead him away.

123

Talking Head: Owen Fallowfield

Another notable triumph among the new characters is Dr
Carlton, a despotic GP who rules his patients with eccentric zeal (3.1).
In appearance, he resembles the serial killer Dr Harold Shipman, but
his manner is that of another surgical practitioner. The documentary
A Change of Sex (BBC2, 1979, 1994, 1999), about George Roberts's
transition to Julia Grant, had yielded plentiful opportunities for
Pemberton and Shearsmith (Carlton's creators) to generate comedy by
recontextualising phrases heard on television as well as in real life,
pushing verbal capsules of aggression or delusion to extremes.[154]
Carlton's inspiration is George/Julia's dour, uncaring psychiatrist, who
had already provided Edward with one of his funniest expressions, 'Is
his identity known?' Carlton's catchphrase is his inspiration's strangely
aggressive dismissal 'Go out, would you' and the sketch builds on this
doctor–patient tyranny. In her efforts to get prescription painkillers,
Mrs Beasley is constantly checked by an arcane and mystifying
etiquette. 'You cannot buy my opinion as you would buy a used motor
car', Carlton snaps when she suggests private treatment. When she
breaks down in tears, he slowly places a Polo mint in his mouth and
crunches it; he's 'broken' her. He leers, satisfied that her pain is

124

'Go out, would you' – Dr Carlton and the Polo mint

'genuine'. She will come to his house as a private patient, alone and with pyjamas for an overnight stay. The payoff is to literalise the infantile nature of Carlton's power play: patients must compete for treatment by playing children's games. 'He makes his own problems', he concludes of a sick boy he sends home when he's eliminated from 'Grandma's Footsteps'.

In one of the most interesting critiques of *The League of Gentlemen*, Ben Thompson sees the transition from sketch to longer narratives as a 'creative blind alley', with the 'tenderness' he discerns in earlier material 'seeping away when the storylines are extended'.[155] Like some of the Amazon reviewers, he also detects a callous feel to series three and suggests that it sacrifices some of its characters 'on the altar of heartlessness'.[156] As a general summation, I can't say that I agree with this. Thompson cites Ross's treatment of Pauline, manipulating and blackmailing her, and then threatening to tell Mickey about their impulse fuck. Episode 3.1 may leave her hanging, but the alleged callousness of Pauline's fate isn't borne out by the climax of the series where, not only does she make it to the altar with Mickey, but Ross arrives at the church and gives a conciliatory wave. Seemingly

125

Happy endings: Pauline marries Mickey

Ross's conciliatory wave

irredeemable Lance finds a kind of redemption in sacrifice (the local
newspaper brands him a hero); Geoff is as content as he's ever likely to
be, getting laughs at last; Alvin exchanges 'rude food' for barbecues,
even though his happiness is at Sunny's expense. Nevertheless, there are
instances where Thompson's comments ring true. Charlie's episode can
be seen as building to a resolution that stresses cruelty at the expense of
comedy. When Charlie confesses his feelings for (and carnal knowledge
of) Tony in a restaurant toilet, he is beaten up.

Dean Tavalouris is another matter, a would-be magician with
a Yorkshire-American accent, volcanic spots, 'milk bottle' glasses and
an odd line in sub-David Blaine patter ('I am he called Dean'). Dean
originated as Simon McCulloch, the intended central character of
episode 3.6, victim of the blackmail plot planned as the linking
narrative. All four Gents appear to have had a hand in developing the
character, but someone (or possibly everyone) seems to have lost track
of the tone of the material; Dyson describes the character's
development as 'tortured ... we just couldn't nail (him)'. In *The Logic
of the Absurd*, Jerry Palmer cites as an example of 'comic failure' (for
him, at least) the 'victimisation' of hippy Neil in *The Young Ones*

(BBC2, 1982–4): 'My personal reaction was to feel that this was simultaneously surprising and also very plausible. I could not see that it was absurd, and it seemed only cruel and therefore unfunny.'[157] I don't share Palmer's reaction to Neil – the cartoon violence seems to keep things safely absurd – but his comments capture my own unease about Dean. As he tries to impress a couple of girls with a disappearing cigarette, two intimidating boys spot the trick and stub the cigarette out on Dean's hand, causing him to scream in pain. As he shrieks at them not to touch his video camera (which they steal), they dissolve into nasty laughter. My problem is not knowing how I'm meant to react to this nastiness. It certainly isn't funny, unless one is nostalgic for a former career as a school bully, but there is no sense, either, of pathos about Dean (unlike, say, Les or Geoff, whose suffering means something).

Another new character, Neds, risks a similar reaction. Neds, too, looks like he would have a target on him in a school playground, ginger-haired and 'boss-eyed'. But there is a stronger comic idea at the centre of this material, one that *Viz* used to delight in; the conceits of children's stories (solving crimes in the school holidays)

127

Dean Tavalouris and the cigarette

colliding with brutal reality. Neds has built a *Knight Rider*-style car called Maxie-Power that fires paper clips ineffectually at a vicious gang of crooks. Beaten senseless, he is left to die in a burning warehouse with his schoolboy sidekick. Ultimately, though, Dean's comic 'failure' (for me) is most thrown into relief by another comic victim, the childlike Barry Baggs. Barry, too, is unflatteringly drawn. Obese and ruddy-cheeked, permanently breathless and hungry, his voice a high-pitched sing-song, he is as ineffectual a debt collector as one could imagine ('Don't say that – you'll scare her!') After an old woman not only sees off the Baggs brothers, but gets them to pay for a broken plant pot, they are summoned to see their ferocious boss. Lisgoe is physical harm incarnate, with slicked-back hair, razor-slashed eyebrow, a tattoo on his neck and a sneering Mancunian accent. They role-play a debt-collecting scene, which builds to a terrible beating from Lisgoe's belt that makes the trailer rock from side to side and Barry howl in terror. Nevertheless, the absurdity is maintained not only by Barry's inability to recognise danger, giggling, ticklish, when Lisgoe tries to get money from his pockets, but by the fact that that which does not kill him does, ridiculously, make him stronger. 'Right!' he shrieks, rising from the

128

Barry beaten by Lisgoe

That which does not kill us ... Barry reborn

thrashing he's just received, ready for his next collection. A polite old
lady immediately agrees to pay, but Barry has become a veritable
juggernaut intent on harm.

129

Returning to the comparison with Python, it's tempting to see
series three as a rough equivalent to *Ripping Yarns*. This might seem like
a rather abstract or eccentric comparison, given that they are very
different in tone, and that the Christmas Special shows the influence of
Palin and Jones more directly. The similarity is in their reception, and
the apparent reasons for that reception, partly determined by the burden
of expectation. In *Ripping Yarns'* case, Python established the
expectations, and the 'Cycling Tour' had been an experiment with an
episode-length narrative. Both series stress atmosphere, richness of
detail and narrative over gag-rate, each is slightly uneven but with some
'classic' episodes and sequences standing out. Both series received a
distinctly mixed reception on their original transmission, sometimes
being seen as disappointing in comparison with earlier work, slightly
self-indulgent and in need of a few more jokes, but the years (and DVD)
have been kind to both. Nevertheless, there's also the sense of something
winding down by the end of series three of *The League of Gentlemen*.

Full circle – Barbara's babies in the final shot

A closing montage offers an elegiac sense of closure: Pauline and Mickey married as Ross looks on, Geoff finally finding an appreciative audience; Barbara's twin babies sporting familiar porcine snouts. Closure, but as the final shot suggests, also circularity. Vasey may seem a very different place since we arrived with Benjamin, but it is still Local.

Postscript: Escape from Royston Vasey?

There's a scene in *The League of Gentlemen's Apocalypse* where Herr Lipp, dragged into the 'real' world where he poses as 'Steve Pemberton', finds a collection of memorabilia and press cuttings in his creator's home. A quote leaps off the page at him woundingly: ' "it would be great to kill them all off!" laughs Gatiss.' Gatiss had indeed said something like this in an interview:

> And what, bizarre though it may sound, if one of those characters suddenly became hugely, implausibly popular. What if they found themselves responsible for another Loadsamoney, or a deformed, sexually troubled Mr Bean? They ponder the scenario. 'Then we'd kill them,' Gatiss replies with a broad, innocent smile. 'Without a shadow of doubt. Whoever they were, as soon as we could, we'd kill them.'[158]

Such statements can come back to haunt us, just as the inhabitants of Vasey haunt their creators in *Apocalypse*. Tubbs and Edward would undergo an ongoing cycle of death and resurrection that has continued beyond series three. *Apocalypse* is a rare creation not only by being an accomplished film based on a British TV comedy, but in managing to be clever, resonant and funny; a film about the problem of turning a series into something fans will recognise without simply padding out a thirty-minute format by taking its characters on holiday to Spain. It also

finds the League at odds with their characters, and while the film sides
with the latter, the Gents portrayed as heartless careerists, it is also
about consigning them to history before moving on to new projects.
In fact, the film appears to have started as an abortive attempt to do
something entirely new, like its film-within-a-film *The King's Evil*.
Apocalypse can be seen as either a dignified send-off or a way of keeping
the League's options open; the characters are kept on literal life support
by a comatose Dyson (played by Michael Sheen).

As it turned out, *Apocalypse* was not the final visit to Vasey. It
would take a harder heart than mine to begrudge the League the raucous
orgy of catchphrases that was their touring semi-panto, *The League of
Gentlemen Are behind You* (2005–6). If the film was ambitious as well
as enjoyable, this was a simpler crowd-pleaser, and a rather patchy one,
if brilliantly staged and performed. There were some undoubted gems
from Geoff, Les, Dr Carlton, Mick McNamara, even Dean (funnier as a
variety turn). But while I still smile at the spectacle of Pauline, in an Ugly
Sister dress that resembled a vindictive Christmas decoration, singing
'It's Raining Pens', a more sober appraisal might conclude that a barrel
was in danger of being scraped. Moreover, by touring at the same time
as a peaking *Little Britain*, the League once again found themselves
compared with British comedy's new 'golden boys'.

Like Python and others before them, the League's influence on
subsequent comedy has been both positive and negative. The best of
what might be seen as post-League shows is *The Mighty Boosh*, which
may not be consciously influenced by the series but shares with it a high
level of production design and the creation of a 'completely furnished
world' for its characters. On the other hand, *Tittybangbang*, a jaw-
dropping car wreck of a sketch show, is clearly performed by gifted
comic actors, but extracts only the grotesqueness of its predecessor and
has none of its wit or invention.

At the time of writing, the League of Gentlemen are on
extended sabbatical, pursuing solo projects. Gatiss undoubtedly has the
highest profile, as a successful novelist, key figure in the revived *Doctor
Who* and a character actor who seems to have his pick of rewarding

character parts. As the non-actor of the team, Dyson has generally had a slightly lower profile, but he, too, is an acclaimed (if very different) novelist and brought his distinctive voice (and obsessions) to *Funland*.[159] *The Cicerones* showed him to be a promising director who might take the reins from Steve Bendelack at some future point. His creative future seems both intriguing and unpredictable. Pemberton and Shearsmith are formidable comic writers and so it's been slightly disappointing to see them work only as character actors for hire away from the League. Both have enjoyed some good parts, in *Blackpool* (BBC, 2004) and *Catterick*, for example, but have sometimes seemed to be punching below their weight in more routine TV productions or poor sitcoms like *The Abbey* (Channel 4, 2007). It's encouraging, then, that they are preparing a series of their own, provisionally titled *Psychoville* and co-funded by HBO. Personally, I hope the League have departed from Royston Vasey for good – it seems to have run its course. But the League of Gentlemen, the team rather than the series, clearly have many exciting things to offer, both individually and hopefully together.

Notes

1 Alison Graham, 'Are You Local?', *Radio Times*, 8–14 January 2000, pp. 28–9.
2 Mark Gatiss, interview with the author, 17 September 2007.
3 *The Vesuvius Club* (London, New York, Sydney, Toronto and Dublin: Simon and Schuster, 2004) has an Edwardian setting, while *The Devil in Amber* (London, New York, Sydney, Toronto and Dublin: Simon and Schuster, 2006) is set between World Wars I and II. He has written two episodes of *Doctor Who* since its return ('The Unquiet Dead', BBC1, 2005 and 'The Idiot's Lantern', 2006) and played the monster in a third ('The Lazarus Experiment', 2007). He wrote a number of novels and audio plays during the period when *Doctor Who* was off the air.
4 Gatiss spent his childhood near a Victorian psychiatric hospital in County Durham, a biographical detail that remains hard to resist.
5 Henri Bergson, 'Laughter' (1910), in Wylie Sypher (ed.), *Comedy* (New York: Doubleday Anchor Books, 1956), p. 79.
6 Jeremy Dyson, interview with the author, 9 September 2007.
7 Ben Thompson, *Sunshine on Putty: The Golden Age of British Comedy from Vic Reeves to* The Office (London: Harper Perennial, 2004), p. 360.
8 Jeremy Dyson, 'An Everyday Story', *Independent on Sunday*, 15 October 2001.
9 'It was just a "fit" thing, really', says Dyson. 'He was just a different kind of performer to what the three of them were, and he was a very good writer as well. The kind of stuff he and Mark wrote was very different from what ended up as the League.'
10 *The League of Gentlemen* (1960) is actually a remarkably sour film about a group of ex-army men staging a bank robbery.
11 A performance that included Stephen Fry, Hugh Laurie, Tony Slattery and Emma Thompson.
12 According to Gatiss, 'Steve never really directed us as actors. We always took care of that ourselves', but he was very important to the look of the series.
13 John O. Thompson, *Monty Python: Complete and Utter Theory of the Grotesque* (London: BFI, 1982), p. 35
14 Jim Sangster and Paul Condon, *TV Heaven* (London: HarperCollins, 2005), p. 489.
15 Roger Wilmut, *From Fringe to Flying Circus: Celebrating a Unique Generation of Comedy 1960–1980* (London: Methuen, 1980), p. 207
16 In *Sunshine on Putty*, Thompson sees it as *the* Golden Age, but I'm more inclined to see it as *a* Golden Age.
17 In the week ending 24 January 1999, the League and *Bang, Bang* got around 2 million, *Gimme,Gimme, Gimme* 3.89 million, but *Red Dwarf* got over 5 million.
18 Python's live shows established an enduring format for a TV show translating to the stage: a raucous 'greatest hits' package.
19 Georgina Born, *Uncertain Vision: Birt, Dyke and the Reinvention of the BBC* (London: Secker and Warburg, 2004), p. 473.
20 'We didn't want to go on BBC Choice', says Gatiss. 'We thought it was like a demotion.'
21 Marcia Landy, *Monty Python's Flying Circus* (Detroit, MI: Wayne State University Press, 2005), p. 28.

22 Rudolf Rocker is its name.

23 Roger Wilmut and Peter Rosengard, *Didn't You Kill My Mother in Law? The Story of Alternative Comedy in Britain from the Comedy Store to Saturday Live* (London: Methuen, 1989), p. xiii.

24 Ibid., p. 21.

25 Thompson, *Sunshine on Putty*, p. 8.

26 Ibid., p. 363.

27 Alison Graham, 'Comedy, the New Drama', *Radio Times*, 5–11 October 2002, p. 69.

28 David J. Skal, *The Monster Show: A Cultural History of Horror* (London: Plexus, 1993), p. 264.

29 J. L. Styan, *The Dark Comedy: The Development of Modern Comic-Tragedy* (London and New York: Cambridge University Press, 1968), p. 289.

30 Skal, *The Monster Show* (citing Albert Goldman), p. 264.

31 Wilmut, *From Fringe to Flying Circus*, p. 213.

32 Bergson, 'Laughter', pp. 63–4.

33 On stage, the sweep of a torch indicates its phallic dimensions, while on radio, we are left to work out the gag for ourselves. On TV, the gag seems to fall victim to the demands of a 'visual medium'.

34 Daniel Rosenthal, 'What's All This Shouting?', *The Times*, 2 March 2001.

35 Brian Viner, *Independent*, 6 February 2000.

36 Geoff King, *Film Comedy* (London: Wallflower, 2002), p.190.

37 'Ungentlemanly Conduct: League Rapped over Language', *Chortle: The UK Comedy Guide*, <www.chortle.co.uk/news/july01/gents html>.

38 Umberto Eco, '*Casablanca*: Cult Movies and Intertextual Collage', in *Travels in Hyper-Reality* (London: Picador, 1987), p. 198.

39 *The League of Gentlemen: Scripts and That* (London: BBC Books, 2003), p. 10.

40 Ibid.

41 Emma Perry, 'Charm Offensive', *Time Out*, 6–13 January 1999, p. 20.

42 Matt Hills, *Fan Cultures* (London and New York: Routledge, 2002), p.144.

43 So called because it is where Mike tells Geoff the 'bummers are deaf' joke.

44 Amy Sergeant, 'Making and Selling Heritage Culture: Style and Authenticity in Historical Fictions on Film and Television', in Justine Ashby and Andrew Higson (eds), *British Cinema: Past and Present* (London and New York: Routledge, 2000), p. 309.

45 Roz Kaveney, *From Alien to The Matrix: Reading Science Fiction Film* (London: I. B. Tauris, 2005), p. 5.

46 David Richardson, 'Special Stuff and Precious Things', *Ultimate DVD* 49 (2003), p. 26.

47 *Scripts and That* provides the answer to the former and a clue to the latter, but I think it best not to say here.

48 Sara Gwenllian Jones, 'Starring Lucy Lawless?', *Continuum: Journal of Media and Cultural Studies* vol. 14 no. 1 (2000), p. 13.

49 Alison Graham, 'Pick of the Day', *Radio Times*, 9–15 January 1999, p. 90.

50 Steve Neale and Frank Krutnik, *Popular Film and Television Comedy* (London and New York: Routledge, 1990), p. 192.

51 Ingleby cameos (off screen) as the world's smallest escapologist in the Pandemonium Carnival (2.1).

52 Although derived from a stage character, Barbara Kadabra, a transsexual stage magician.

53 Wilmut, *From Fringe to Flying Circus*, p. 220. Dyson has described Chinnery as a 'Palin *Monty Python* character' (Rosenthal, 'What's All This Shouting?').

54 The League call this gesture a 'Manning' on the DVD commentary, after the club comedian's method of wiping sweat from his face.

135

55 A 'briss' is a Jewish circumcision ritual.
56 'I find myself described as "This Northern lad" – Is Pinter ever described as "This East End boy"?', quoted by Katie Wales, *Northern English: A Social and Cultural History* (Cambridge: Cambridge University Press, 2006), p. 29.
57 Rob Shields, *Places on the Margin: Alternative Geographies of Modernity* (London and New York: Routledge, 1991), pp. 207–8.
58 *In Conversation with The League of Gentlemen*, Radio 4 2002.
59 Simon Morgan-Russell, 'A Local Shop for Local People: Imbrication and Alienation in British Situation Comedy', *Journal of British Cinema and Television* vol. 4 no. 2 (2007), p. 330.
60 Andrew Higson, 'Space, Place, Spectacle: Landscape and Townscape in the "Kitchen Sink" Film', in A. Higson (ed.), *Dissolving Views: Rethinking British Cinema* (London and New York: Cassell, 1996), p. 152.
61 Shields, *Places on the Margin*, p. 221.
62 Terry Lovell, 'Landscapes and Stories in 1960s' British Realism', in Higson (ed.), *Dissolving Views*, p. 171.
63 For more on 'liminal northernness', see Wales, *Northern English*, pp. 141–51
64 Jeremy Dyson, 'An Everyday Story'.
65 Jeff Nuttall and Rodick Carmichael, *Common Factors/Vulgar Factions* (London, Henley and Boston: Routledge and Kegan Paul, 1977), p. 24.
66 Ibid., p. 24.
67 Roy 'Chubby' Brown, *Common as Muck! My Autobiography* (London: Sphere, 2007), p. 360.
68 Nuttall and Carmichael, *Common Factors*, p. 38.
69 Ibid., pp. 34–5.
70 Ibid., p. 36.
71 Ibid., p. 37.
72 Wilmut, *From Fringe to Flying Circus*, p. 100.
73 Ibid., p. 93
74 Laraine Porter, 'Tarts, Tampons and Tyrants: Women and Representation in British Comedy', in Steve Wagg (ed.), *Because I Tell a Joke or Two: Comedy, Politics and Social Difference* (London and New York: Routledge, 1998), p. 84.
75 George Orwell, 'The Art of Donald McGill' (1941), in *Decline of the English Murder and Other Essays* (Harmondsworth: Penguin, 1965), p. 145.
76 Porter, 'Tarts, Tampons and Tyrants', p. 90.
77 Ibid., p. 91.
78 *100 Greatest TV Characters* (Channel 4, 2001). Tubbs was number 16 on the list.
79 Or might not – Mike's wedding juggles a fair few characters.
80 Theodor Dalrymple, 'A Horror Story', <www.cityjournal.org/html/6_2_oh_to_be.html>.
81 Rosenthal, 'What's All This Shouting?'.
82 Peter Hutchings, 'Uncanny Landscapes in British Film and Television', *Visual Culture in Great Britain* vol. 5 no. 2 (2004), p. 35.
83 Ibid., p. 35.
84 *Scripts and That*, p. 19.
85 One's gothic destiny is rather predetermined by a name like 'Radclyffe'.
86 See, for example, Andy Medhurst, 'Negotiating the Gnome Zone: Versions of Suburbia in British Popular Culture', in Roger Silverstone (ed.), *Visions of Suburbia* (London and New York: Routledge, 1997).
87 Mary Douglas, *Purity and Danger: An Analysis of Pollution and Taboo* (London and New York: Routledge, 1991), p. 2.
88 Ibid., p. 38.
89 Dyson, 'An Everyday Story'.
90 Mark Morris (ed.), *Cinema Macabre* (Hornsea: PS Publishing, 2006),

pp. 99–102. Dyson also contributed to
Cinema Macabre, characteristically picking
a classic from the tradition of restraint and
suggestion, *Night of the Demon* (1957).
91 Peter Hutchings, 'The Amicus House of
Horror', in Steve Chibnall and Julian Petley
(eds), *British Horror Cinema* (London and
New York: Routledge, 2002), p. 242.
92 Helen Wheatley, *Gothic Television*
(Manchester: Manchester University Press,
2006), p. 66.
93 Dyson injects a lascivious relish into the
line 'Haiti? How … *exotic*' and rises to some
maniacal laughter at the end. *Highgate
House of Horror* is included complete on the
Japanese DVD of the Christmas Special –
clearance of the music cues seems to have
reduced it to clips on the UK Region 2 and
US Region 1 versions.
94 One might also cite *The Simpsons'*
annual Halloween *Treehouse of Horror*
specials, starting in 1990. They share with
the League's Christmas Special a non-
canonical 'bubble' that allows the
supernatural into the series.
95 Gatiss guest-stars as 'The Sinister Bony-
Fingered Menace from the East', the
nemesis of Coogan's Jason King-like hero,
Nathan Blaze.
96 Available at <www.amazon.co.uk/
League-Gentlemen-Christmas-Special/dp/
B00006JY8N/ref=sr_1_9/202-2142728-
6627064?ie=UTF8&s=dvd&qid=
1180082211&sr=1-9>.
97 *The Same Dog* was performed as an
oratorio at the Barbican in 2000, with
music by Joby Talbot, while Dyson co-
adapted *Ringing the Changes* (Radio 4,
2001) with Gatiss.
98 For example, Denis Gifford, *A Pictorial
History of Horror Movies* (London, New York,
Sydney and Toronto: Hamlyn, 1973), Alan
Frank, *Horror Movies: Tales of Terror in the
Cinema* (London: Octopus, 1974).

99 Wheatley, *Gothic Television*, pp. 90–121.
100 Ibid., p. 8.
101 Ibid., p. 88.
102 Available at <www.channel4.com/film/
newsfeatures/microsites/S/scary/results_
30-21_2.html>.
103 Jeffrey Sconce, *Haunted Media:
Electronic Presence from Telegraph to
Television* (Durham, NC and London: Duke
University Press, 2000).
104 Gatiss's first *Doctor Who* novel
Nightshade makes more explicit reference
to *Quatermass*.
105 Catherine Johnson, *Telefantasy*
(London: BFI, 2005), pp. 19–41.
106 Sigmund Freud, 'The Uncanny (Das
Unheimlich)', in *Art and Literature*
(Harmondsworth: Penguin, 1985).
107 Cited by Wheatley, *Gothic Television*,
p. 71.
108 Mikhail Bakhtin, *Rabelais and His
World* (Bloomington: Indiana University
Press, 1984), p. 276.
109 Peter Hutchings, 'Welcome to Royston
Vasey: Grotesque Bodies and the Horror of
Comedy in *The League of Gentlemen*',
Intensities no. 4 (2007), p. 7, available at
<www.intensities.org/Essays/Hutchings.pdf>.
110 Michael Steig, 'Defining the Grotesque:
An Attempt at Synthesis', *Journal of
Aesthetics and Art Criticism* no. 29 (1970),
p. 259.
111 Ibid., p. 258.
112 Ibid., p. 258.
113 Ibid., p. 260.
114 William Paul, *Laughing Screaming:
Modern Hollywood Horror and Comedy* (New
York: Columbia University Press, 1994),
p. 419.
115 His racial ambiguity – voice based
on a Greek landlord, skin tone assumed
to be artificial – becomes more disturbing
in series three when the 'blackface'
proves to be his natural hue, like the

unnaturally white skin of the Joker in
Batman.

116 'A Little Local Difficulty', *Guardian*, 28
December 2000.

117 Gatiss: 'When Reece is doing that
character, there's something terrible going on
– something primal' (Tom Spilsbury, 'Out of
this League', *Ultimate DVD* no. 36, p. 32).

118 Freud found in a number of ancient
myths a father figure who kept all of the
women for himself and was feared and
envied by the sons who banded together to
destroy and devour him: *Totem and Taboo*
(London and New York: Routledge, 2001).

119 The Santa guise alludes to 'And All
through the House', a story that first
appeared in EC Comics' *Vault of Horror*
no. 35 (1954). It was adapted for Amicus's
Tales from the Crypt in 1972, with Joan
Collins menaced by a homicidal maniac in a
Santa suit on Christmas Eve.

120 David Miller, 'Gentlemen's Relish',
Shivers no. 100 (November 2002), p. 20.

121 The League's unofficial title for the
Christmas Special.

122 For which observation I am indebted to
the Christmas Special fan commentary at
<tv.groups.yahoo.com/group/the_League_
of_Gentlemen/files/Articles>.

123 Should we be surprised that League-
themed slash fiction often casts Reece
Shearsmith as 'The Eternal Victim', tied up
and tormented?

124 Nigel Kneale's adaptation of *The
Woman in Black* (Central, 1989) was a
particular influence, as was the TV movie of
Salem's Lot (Warner Brothers/CBS, 1979).

125 Wheatley, *Gothic Television*,
pp. 42–55.

126 David Punter and Glennis Byron, *The
Gothic* (Malden, MA, Oxford and Carlton,
Victoria: Blackwell, 2006), p. 48.

127 The name derives from one of the
puppets in children's TV show *The Pipkins*

(ATV, 1973–81), best remembered for the
extraordinarily camp Hartley Hare.

128 Introduction to 'The Unquiet Dead' in
Doctor Who: The Shooting Scripts (London:
BBC Books, 2005), p. 90.

129 *The League of Gentlemen: A Local Book
for Local People* (London: Fourth Estate,
2000).

130 Gatiss, *The Vesuvius Club*, p. 127.

131 Wilmut, *From Fringe to Flying Circus*,
p. 251.

132 Christmas Specials seem to count as
permissible extras.

133 Gatiss concurred with this theory.

134 *Observer*, 9 January 2000.

135 *Daily Telegraph*, 27 September 2002.

136 *Guardian*, 27 September 2002.

137 *Radio Times*, 26 October–1 November
2002, (2002) p. 108.

138 See <www.amazon.co.uk/gp/product/
customer-reviews/B00004WZYQ/sr=1-2/
qid=1187945798/ref=cm_rev_prev/202-
4651775-8243802?ie=UTF8&customer-
reviews.sort%5Fby=-SubmissionDate&n=
573398&s=video&customer-reviews.
start=1&qid=1187945798&sr=1-2>.

139 Available at <www.amazon.co.uk/gp/
product/customer-reviews/B0000D9Y9S/
sr=1-10/qid=1187946753/ref=cm_rev_
next/202-4651775-8243802?ie=
UTF8&customer-reviews.sort%5Fby=-
SubmissionDate&n=283926&s=
dvd&customer-reviews.start=41&qid=
1187946753&sr=1-10>.

140 See <www.amazon.co.uk/gp/product/
customer-reviews/B0000D9Y9S/sr=1-10/
qid=1187946753/ref=cm_rev_prev/202-
4651775-8243802?ie=UTF8&customer-
reviews.sort%5Fby=-SubmissionDate&n=
283926&s=dvd&customer-reviews.start=
11&qid=1187946753&sr=1-10>.

141 I suspect, though, that this is less the
result of mean-spiritedness than the need to
get him to the site of the accident – the

joined-up ending is sometimes a bit of a burden in later episodes.

142 Nick Joy, 'Joby Talbot: The *Hitchhiker's Guide to the Galaxy*', *Music from the Movies* (2007), <www.musicfromthemovies.com/sotw.asp?ID=36>.

143 Jacob Smith, 'The Frenzy of the Audible: Pleasure, Authenticity and Recorded Laughter', *Television and New Media* vol. 6 no. 1 (2005), p. 37.

144 Ibid., pp. 39–40.

145 Brett Mills, *Television Sitcom* (London: BFI, 2005), p. 51.

146 Karen Lury, *Interpreting Television* (London: Hodder Arnold, 2005), p. 83.

147 The series is full of this kind of 'continuity'. In prison with Pauline is Maurice's wife Eunice, responsible for 'cutting' the Special Stuff. Brian encounters Lazarou when he investigates the disappearance of his (and Geoff's former) wife. This possibly didn't help the series pick up new viewers, although as Gatiss observed when I made this point, most of the narratives don't stand or fall on these fannish details.

148 *Daily Telegraph*, 27 September 2002.

149 *Scripts and That*, p. 207.

150 Worn, Gatiss tells me, as a result of an autoerotic incident with a flex.

151 Tanya Krzywinska, *A Skin for Dancing In: Possession, Witchcraft and Voodoo in Film* (Trowbridge: Flicks Books, 2000), p. 67.

152 Cited by Eve Kosofsky Sedgwick, *Between Men: English Literature and Male Homosocial Desire* (New York: Columbia University Press), p. 21.

153 Ibid., p. 1.

154 It's one of Pemberton's choices in *The League of Gentlemen's Book of Precious Things* (London: Prion Books, 2007), an anthology of influences.

155 Thompson, *Sunshine on Putty*, p. 368.

156 Ibid., p. 369.

157 Jerry Palmer, *The Logic of the Absurd* (London: BFI, 1987), p. 137.

158 Danny Leigh, 'Comic Geniuses', *Guardian*, 14 January 2000.

159 'I remember Mark (Gatiss) saying after *Funland* that he could see what all my obsessions were – seedy landlords, pornography, depravity.'

Select Bibliography

Bergson, Henri, 'Laughter', in Wylie Sypher (ed.), *Comedy* (New York: Doubleday Anchor Books, 1956).

Born, Georgina, *Uncertain Vision: Birt, Dyke and the Reinvention of the BBC* (London: Secker and Warburg, 2004).

Caldwell, John Thornton, *Televisuality: Style, Crisis and Authority in American Television* (New Brunswick, NJ: Rutgers University Press, 1995).

Creeber, Glen (ed.), *The Television Genre Book* (London: BFI, 2001).

Douglas, Mary, *Purity and Danger: An Analysis of Pollution and Taboo* (London and New York: Routledge, 1991).

Dyson, Jeremy, *Bright Darkness: The Lost Art of the Supernatural Horror Film* (London and Washington: Cassell, 1997).

Dyson, Jeremy, *Never Trust a Rabbit* (London: Duckbacks, 2000).

Dyson, Jeremy, 'Shadows and Fog', *Guardian* (30 January 2004), <www.guardian.co.uk/arts/fridayreview/story/0,12102,1134055,00.html>.

Dyson, Jeremy, *What Happens Now* (London: Abacus, 2006).

Dyson, Jeremy and Gatiss, Mark, *The Essex Files: To Basildon and Beyond* (London: Fourth Estate, 1997).

Dyson, Jeremy, Gatiss, Mark, Pemberton, Steve and Shearsmith, Reece, *The League of Gentlemen: A Local Book for Local People* (London: Fourth Estate, 2000).

Dyson, Jeremy, Gatiss, Mark, Pemberton, Steve and Shearsmith, Reece, *The League of Gentlemen: Scripts and That* (London: BBC Books, 2003).

Dyson, Jeremy, Gatiss, Mark, Pemberton, Steve and Shearsmith, Reece, *The League of Gentlemen's Book of Precious Things* (London: Prion Books, 2007).

Easthope, Anthony, *Englishness and National Culture* (London and New York: Routledge, 1999).

Eco, Umberto, '*Casablanca*: Cult Movies and Intertextual Collage', in *Travels in Hyper-Reality* (London: Picador, 1987).

Gatiss, Mark, *Nightshade* (London: Virgin/Doctor Who Books, 1992).

Gatiss, Mark, *St Anthony's Fire* (London: Virgin/Doctor Who Books, 1994).

Gatiss, Mark, *James Whale: A Biography* (London and New York: Cassell, 1995).

Gatiss, Mark, *Doctor Who: The Roundheads* (London: BBC Books, 1997).

Gatiss, Mark, *Doctor Who: Last of the Gadarene* (London: BBC Books, 2000).

Gatiss, Mark, *The Vesuvius Club* (London, New York, Sydney, Toronto and Dublin: Simon and Schuster, 2004).

Gatiss, Mark, 'The Unquiet Dead', in *Doctor Who: The Shooting Scripts* (London: BBC Books, 2005).

Gatiss, Mark, *The Devil in Amber* (London, New York, Sydney, Toronto and Dublin: Simon and Schuster, 2006).

Hall, Julian, *The Rough Guide to British Cult Comedy* (London and New York: Rough Guides/Penguin, 2006).

Higson, Andrew, 'Space, Place, Spectacle: Landscape and Townscape in the "Kitchen Sink" Film', in Andrew Higson (ed.), *Dissolving Views: Rethinking British Cinema* (London and New York: Cassell, 1996).

Hills, Matt, *Fan Cultures* (London and New York: Routledge, 2002).

Horner, Avril and Zlosnik, Sue, 'Comic Gothic', in David Punter (ed.), *A Companion to the Gothic* (Malden, MA, Oxford and Carlton, Victoria: Blackwell, 2001).

Hutchings, Peter, 'The Amicus House of Horror', in Steve Chibnall and Julian Petley (eds), *British Horror Cinema* (London and New York: Routledge, 2002).

Hutchings, Peter, 'Uncanny Landscapes in British Film and Television', *Visual Culture in Great Britain* vol. 5 no. 2 (2004).

Hutchings, Peter, 'Welcome to Royston Vasey: Grotesque Bodies and the Horror of Comedy in *The League of Gentlemen*', *Intensities* no. 4 (2007), available at <www.intensities.org/Essays/Hutchings.pdf>.

Jacobson, Howard, *Seriously Funny: From the Ridiculous to the Sublime* (London: Viking, 1997).

Johnson, Catherine, *Telefantasy* (London: BFI, 2005).

Kaveney, Roz, *From Alien to The Matrix: Reading Science Fiction Film* (London: I. B. Tauris, 2005).

King, Geoff, *Film Comedy* (London: Wallflower, 2002).

Krzywinska, Tanya, *A Skin for Dancing In: Possession, Witchcraft and Voodoo in Film* (Trowbridge: Flicks Books, 2000).

Krzywinska, Tanya, 'Lurking beneath the Skin: Identity, Magic and the English Pagan Landscape in the Popular Imagination', in Robert Fish (ed.), *Cinematic Countrysides* (Manchester: Manchester University Press, 2007).

Landy, Marcia, *Monty Python's Flying Circus* (Detroit, MI: Wayne State University Press, 2005).

Lovell, Terry, 'Landscapes and Stories in 1960s' British Realism', in Andrew Higson (ed.), *Dissolving Views: Rethinking British Cinema* (London and New York: Cassell, 1996).

Lury, Karen, *Interpreting Television* (London: Hodder Arnold, 2005).

Medhurst, Andy, 'Negotiating the Gnome Zone: Versions of Suburbia in British Popular Culture', in Roger Silverstone (ed.), *Visions of Suburbia* (London and New York: Routledge, 1977).

Mills, Brett, *Television Sitcom* (London: BFI, 2005).

Morgan-Russell, Simon, 'A Local Shop for Local People: Imbrication and Alienation in British Situation Comedy', *Journal of British Cinema and Television* vol. 4 no. 2 (2007).

Morris, Marc (ed.), *Cinema Macabre* (Hornsea: PS Publishing, 2006).

Neale, Steve and Krutnik, Frank, *Popular Film and Television Comedy* (London and New York: Routledge, 1990).

Nuttall, Jeff and Carmichael, Rodick, *Common Factors/Vulgar Factions* (London, Henley and Boston, MA: Routledge and Kegan Paul, 1977).

Palmer, Jerry, *The Logic of the Absurd* (London: BFI, 1987).

Paul, William, *Laughing Screaming: Modern Hollywood Horror and Comedy* (New York: Columbia University Press, 1994).

Porter, Laraine, 'Tarts, Tampons and Tyrants: Women and Representation in British Comedy', in Steve Wagg (ed.), *Because I Tell a Joke or Two: Comedy, Politics and Social Difference* (London and New York: Routledge, 1998).

Prawer, S. S., *Caligari's Children: The Film as Tale of Terror* (Oxford, New York, Toronto and Melbourne: Oxford University Press, 1980).

141

Punter, David and Byron, Glennis, *The Gothic* (Malden, MA, Oxford and Carlton, Victoria: Blackwell, 2004).

Rigby, Jonathan, *English Gothic. A Century of Horror Cinema* (London: Reynolds and Hearn, 2004).

Sangster, Jim and Condon, Paul, *TV Heaven* (London: HarperCollins, 2005).

Shields, Rob, *Places on the Margin: Alternative Geographies of Modernity* (London and New York: Routledge, 1991).

Skal, David J., *The Monster Show: A Cultural History of Horror* (London: Plexus, 1993).

Smith, Jacob, 'The Frenzy of the Audible: Pleasure, Authenticity and Recorded Laughter', *Television and New Media* vol. 6 no. 1 (2005).

Steig, Michael, 'Defining the Grotesque: An Attempt at Synthesis', *Journal of Aesthetics and Art Criticism* no. 29 (1970).

Styan, J. L., *The Dark Comedy: The Development of Modern Comic-Tragedy* (London and New York: Cambridge University Press, 1968).

Sweet, Matthew, *Inventing the Victorians* (London: Faber, 2001).

Thompson, Ben, *Sunshine on Putty: The Golden Age of British Comedy from Vic Reeves to* The Office (London: Harper Perennial, 2004).

Thompson, John O., *Monty Python: Complete and Utter Theory of the Grotesque* (London: BFI, 1982).

Wales, Katie, *Northern English: A Social and Cultural History* (Cambridge: Cambridge University Press, 2006).

Waller, Gregory A. 'Made-for-Television Horror Films', in Gregory A. Waller (ed.), *American Horrors: Essays on the Modern American Horror Film* (Urbana and Chicago: University of Illinois Press, 1987).

Wheatley, Helen, 'Haunted Houses, Hidden Rooms: Women, Domesticity and the Female Gothic Adaptation on Television', in Jonathan Bignall and Stephen Lacey (eds), *Popular Television Drama: Critical Perspectives* (Manchester and New York: Manchester University Press, 2005).

Wheatley, Helen, *Gothic Television* (Manchester and New York: Manchester University Press, 2006).

Wilmut, Roger, *From Fringe to Flying Circus: Celebrating a Unique Generation of Comedy 1960–1980* (London: Methuen, 1980).

Wilmut, Roger and Rosengard, Peter, *Didn't You Kill My Mother-in-Law? The Story of Alternative Comedy in Britain from the Comedy Store to Saturday Live* (London: Methuen, 1989).

Credits

The League of Gentlemen

League of Gentlemen are
Jeremy Dyson
Mark Gatiss
Steve Pemberton
Reece Shearsmith

series one
(six episodes, BBC2 tx
11/01/1999–15/02/1999)

United Kingdom/1999

directed by
Steve Bendelack
producer
Sarah Smith
written by
the cast
and
Jeremy Dyson
director of photography
Rob Kitzmann
editors
Janey Walkin [1]
Will Yarrow [1]
Adam Windmill [1–6]
Nick McPhee [2–6]
design
Grenville Horner
Sarah Kane
music composed & arranged by
Joby Talbot

©/**production company**
BBC

executive producer
Jon Plowman
associate producer
Jemma Rodgers
production co-ordinator
Katie Tyrrell [1]
production accountant
Alison Passey
locations
Paul Grant
Jim Capper [1]
Brett Wilson [2–6]

studio managers
Brian Abram
Annie Beever
assistant floor manager
Tracy-Jane Read
production assistants
Jane Sprague [1]
Katie Tyrrell [2–6]
assistant directors
Duncan Goudan [Gaudin] [1]
Jonathan Leather [1]
Jon Garbett [1]
Ben Rothwell [2–6]
Lydia Currie [2–6]
lighting camera
Peter Edwards
studio camera
Matt Ingham
second unit camera
Paul Lilley [4]
camera assistants
Kevin White [1]
Bil [Bill] Ashworth [2, 3, 5, 6]
gaffers
Fritz Henry
Vinny Cowper
grip
Andy Young
visual effects
Evan Green-Hughes [1–4, 6]
Mark Danbury [1–4, 6]
optical effects
Framestore
vision mixer
Carol Abbott
vision engineer
Stan Robinson
property buyer
Ian Tulley [Tully]
properties
Dickon Peschek [1]
Rob Sellers [1]
Darren Wisker [1]
Trevor Daniels [2–6]
Eric Levey [2–6]
Simon Buret [2–6]

costume
Yves Barre
Scott Langridge
Amanda Hooley
make-up & hair
Helen Barrett [1]
Sarah Crispo [1]
Pippa Hindle [1]
Vanessa White [2–6]
Jules Francis [2–6]
Martine Randall [2–6]
location sound
David Hall
Ben Brookes
studio sound
Chris Greaves
dubbing mixers
Chris Burdon
Rick Williams
Peter Gates
animal handler
Pat Powell [1–4, 6]
armourer
Les Powell [1–3, 5, 6]

cast
Mark Gatiss
Steve Pemberton
Reece Shearsmith

also featuring

1 welcome to Royston Vasey
Frances Cox
Mike Flanagan
Edward McCracken

2 the road to Royston Vasey
Stephen Chapman
Ameet Channa
Colin Parry

3 nightmare in Royston Vasey
Don Estelle
Richard Gardiner
Frances Cox
Amanda Lockett
John Flitcroft

143

4 the beast of Royston Vasey
Don Estelle
Edward McCracken
Keith Ladd
Ian Ralph
Glenn Cunningham
John Flitcroft
John De Main
Megan & Rosy De Wolf
**Glossopdale Community
College**

5 love comes to Royston Vasey
Judith Vause
Ross McCormack
Mike Flanagan
Curtis Watt
Megan & Rosy De Wolf

6 escape from Royston Vasey
Patsy Maguire Crawford
Les Doherty
Thomas Sherlock
Megan & Rosy De Wolf
Ruth Harrop
Myles Hindley

series two
(six episodes, BBC2 tx
14/01/2000–18/02/2000)

United Kingdom/2000

directed by
Steve Bendelack
producer
Jemma Rodgers
written by
Jeremy Dyson
Mark Gatiss
Steve Pemberton
Reece Shearsmith
director of photography
Rob Kitzmann
editors
Peter Hallworth
Adam Windmill
Will Yarrow [1–4, 6]
Andy Wilks [5]
design
Grenville Horner
Sarah Kane
Ruth Winn

music composed & arranged by
Joby Talbot

©/production company
BBC

executive producer
Jon Plowman
assistant producer
Jeremy Dyson
production manager
Stephen Abrahams
locations
Carlene King
Brett Wilson
studio manager
Brian Abram
production assistant
Katie Tyrrell
assistant directors
Duncan Goudin
Liz Summers
Lydia Currie
Sam Leek
location camera
Peter Edwards
second unit
The Camera Crewing Co [3, 4]
gaffer
Fritz Henry
best boy
Alan Walker
grip
Andy Young
visual effects
Evan Green-Hughes
Mark Danbury
vision mixer
Carol Abbott
property buyer
Ian Tully
properties
Trevor Daniels
Noel Deegan
Simon Buret
construction manager
Kevin Waite
costume
Yves Barre
Scott Langridge
Amanda Hooley
make-up & hair
Vanessa White
Helen Johnson
Martine Randall

optical effects
Framestore
music engineer
Mark Whiley [aka Wyllie] [3, 4]
soundtrack
'Voodoo Lady' written by
Rudolf Rocker [5]
location sound
David Hall
Ben Brookes
studio sound
Chris Greaves
dubbing mixers
Nick Fry
Robin Green [6]
animal handler
Pat Ward
armourer
Les Powell [6]

cast
Mark Gatiss
Steve Pemberton
Reece Shearsmith

also featuring

1 destination: Royston Vasey
Rusty Goffe
Gerald Stadden
Jon Key
Paul Popplewell
Johnny Leeze
Frances Cox
John Lebar
Megan & Rosy De Wolfe

2 lust for Royston Vasey
John Draycott
Sian Foulkes
Hope Johnstone
Christine Furness
Martina McClements
Blake Ritson
Laurel Gibb
Megan & Rosy De Wolf
Liam Winston
**Glossopdale Community
College**

3 a plague on Royston Vasey
Laurel Gibb
Jennifer Lim
Chris Freeney

144

Alison Lloyd
Johnny Leeze
Helen Lambert
Victoria Turner

4 death in Royston Vasey
Roy 'Chubby' Brown
Martin Crocker
Blake Ritson
Alan Faulkner
Chris Freeney
Jennifer Lim
Helen Lambert

5 anarchy in Royston Vasey
Judith Vause
Helen Lambert
Johnny Leeze
Ted Robbins
Alison Lloyd
Blake Ritson
John R. Thompson

6 Royston Vasey and the monster from hell
Paul H. Marshall
Roy 'Chubby' Brown
Johnny Leeze
Niall Ross Hogan
Helen Lambert
Jeillo Edwards
Jaqui Ross
Mike Flannagan [Flanagan]
Tim Beasley
Ian Ralph
Edward Wiseman
Martina McClements
Les Doherty
Amanda Lockett
Megan De Wolf
Rosy De Wolf

The League of Gentlemen
(one-off Christmas Special,
BBC2 tx 27/12/2000)

United Kingdom/2000

director
Steve Bendelack
producer
Jemma Rodgers
written by
Jeremy Dyson
Mark Gatiss

Steve Pemberton
Reece Shearsmith
director of photography
Rob Kitzmann
editor
Adam Windmill
production designer
Grenville Horner
music composed & arranged by
Joby Talbot

©/production company
BBC

executive producer
Jon Plowman
assistant producer
Jeremy Dyson
production manager
Alison Passey
locations
Mark Gladwin
Jude Harrison
production assistant
Katie Tyrrell
assistant directors
Carlene King
Anna Brabbins
Sam Leek
cameras
Peter Edwards
Bill Ashworth
Gareth Lowndes
gaffers
Fritz Henry
Alan Walker
grip
Andy Young
visual effects
Evan Green-Hughes
Mark Danbury
Hothouse Models & Effects
art directors
Sarah Kane
Ruth Winn
property buyer
Gemma Ryan
properties
Simon Buret
Noel Deegan
Simon Drew
costume
Yves Barre
Joanna Beatty
Cathy Kirby

make-up & hair
Daniel Phillips
Helen Johnson
Diane Chenery-Wickens
optical effects
Framestore
choreographer
Pat Garrett
sound
David Hall
Ed Brookes
dubbing mixers
Nigel Heath
Michael Fentum
animal handlers
Pat Ward
Les Powell
Steve Dent

cast
Mark Gatiss
Steve Pemberton
Reece Shearsmith
Freddie Jones
Liza Tarbuck
Andrew Melville
Frances Cox
Bay White
Rusty Goffe
Gerald Stadden
Jon Key
Judith Vause
New London Children's Choir
The Royston Vasey Line Dancers

series three
(six episodes, BBC2 tx
26/09/2002–31/10/2002)

United Kingdom/2002

director
Steve Bendelack
producer
Jemma Rodgers
written by
Jeremy Dyson
Mark Gatiss
Steve Pemberton
Reece Shearsmith
director of photography
Rob Kitzmann

145

editors
Adam Windmill
Tony Cranstoun
production design
Grenville Horner
music composed & arranged by
John Talbot

©/production company
BBC

executive producer
Jon Plowman
assistant producer
Jeremy Dyson
production executive
Claire Bridgland
production finance associate
Maz Cooper
production manager
Jill Hallowell
production co-ordinator
Charlotte Lamb
location manager
Carlene King
location assistants
Sam Leek
Andrew Morgan
locations fixer
Chris Woodward
studio manager
Brian Abram
production assistant
Caren Williams
first assistant director
Mel Nortcliffe
assistant directors
Anna Brabbins
Aden Turner
Guy De Glanville
casting adviser
Pam Alexander
location camera operator
Jane Rousseau
camera assistants
Steve Smith
Lil Fletcher
gaffer
Fritz Henry
best boy
David Manfield
grip
Andy Young

visual effects design
Steve Lucas
Jon Savage
vision mixer
Jenny Bozson
art director
Sarah Kane
assistant art directors
Ruth Winn
Robinia Kelly
story board artist
Mike Nicholson
property buyer
Ian Tully
prop master
Trevor Daniels
stand-by props
Noel Deegan
Simon Buret
dressing props
Laurence Archer
Barry Kirkham
construction manager
Kevin Waite
costume design
Yves Barre
costume assistants
Joanna Beatty
Tom Reeve
make-up design
Diane Chenery-Wickens
make-up & hair assistants
Helen Johnson
Xanthia White
optical effects
Framestore-CFC
music engineer
Mark Wyllie [aka Whiley]
sound recordist
David Hall
boom operators
Alison Ross
Lisa Curry
studio sound
Gareth Hall
dubbing mixer
Nigel Heath
sound editor
Dan Morgan
stunt co-ordinator
Rod Woodruff
stuntmen
Andy Smart [2]
Steve Caswell [2]
Paul Kulik [2]

animal handler
Pat Ward [3, 5]
Amazing Animals [6]

cast
Mark Gatiss
Steve Pemberton
Reece Shearsmith

also featuring

1 the lesbian and the monkey
Rosie Clayton
Michael Gallagher
Helen Lambert
Judith Vause

2 the one-armed man is king
Wim Booth
Kevin Brannagan
Sian Foulkes
Michael Gallagher
Sylvie Gattrill
Nicky Goldie
Olivia Jardith
Hope Johnstone
Olive Pendleton

3 turn again, Geoff Tipps
Sally Armstrong
Ilario Bifi-Pedro
Terry Bird
Gordon Cooper
Jason Hall
Cal Jaggers
Barbara Kirby
Andy Nyman
Simon Vigar

4 the Medusa touch
Bhudeb Banerjee
Roger Bingham
Nicholas Briggs
Kate Deakin
Diana Flacks
Chrissie Furness
Michael Gallager [Gallagher]
Alan Gear
Laurence Llewelyn Bowen
Anne Orwin
Olive Pendleton
Alan Strangeway
Brooke Vincent
Sally Womersley

5 beauty and the beast (or, come into my parlour)
Neil Bell
Gary Damer
John De Main
Steve Hillman
Ned Irish
John Jardine
Martina McClements
Roz McCutcheon

6 how the elephant got its trunk
Donna-Marie Dawson
Christopher Eccleston
Belinda Everett
Chris Freeney
Michael Gallager [Gallagher]
Rusty Goffe
Olga Grahame
Andrew Grose
Jon Key
Gordon Langford-Rowe
Jennifer Lim
Paul Oldham
Gerald Stadden
David Williams

production details
'filmed on location with the kind co-operation of the people of Hadfield (High Peak, Derbyshire) and at YTV Studios (Leeds)'

credits compiled by Julian Grainger

147

Index

Notes

Indexing of character names is by first name/epithet (where there is one) and indicates detailed analysis (passing references are not included); page numbers in *italic* denote illustrations or extensively illustrated sections; *n* = endnote.

A

The Abbey 133
The Addams Family 77
Aherne, Caroline 23, 50–2
Aickman, Robert, works adapted by Dyson 77–8
Ainley, Anthony 78
All Creatures Great and Small 66–7
Allen, Dave 99, 103
alternative comedy, definitions/examples 18–24
'Alvin' (character) 116–18
Amazon.co.uk, customer reviews 107
American Beauty (1999) 111
An American Werewolf in London (1981) 66
Amicus Films 76, 92–3
Anderson, Gordon 8–9
The Archers (radio) 64
Atkinson, Rowan 11
awards
  The League of Gentlemen (TV series) 13

B

bad taste/offensiveness
  accusations of 30, 32–3, 107
  in 'dark comedy' 24–6
bad taste/offensiveness *cont.*
  on DVD commentary 38
  in *L of G* 26–33
Baker, Tom 19, 80
Bakhtin, Mikhail 82–3
Bang Bang, It's Reeves and Mortimer 17, 23–4
Bannen, Ian 90–1
'Barbara' (character) 58
Barker, Ronnie 12
Barraclough, Roy 57–8
Barre, Yves 13, 14
Barrett, Helen 14
'Barry' (character) *128*, 128–9, *129*
Beasts 66
Bell, Jamie 38
Bendelack, Steve 13, 19, 96, 133
'Benjamin' (character) 45–6, 49–50, *71*
Bennett, Alan 7, 8, 26, 48, 50–2, 54, 122
Bergson, Henri 4, 26, 83
'Bernice Woodall, Rev.' (character) 88–9, *90*
Beyond the Fringe 21
Blackpool 133
Blaine, David 126
The Blair Witch Project (1999) 63
Blake, Susie 57
Blood on Satan's Claw (1971) 78
Bly, Robert 42
Bo' Selecta 21

Bogarde, Dirk 10
Bradbury, Ray 85
Brand, Russell 20
Brass Eye Special 12
Bretton Hall (college) 3, 5, 8–9
'Brian' (character) 59–64, *60*, *63*
Brown, Roy 'Chubby' 1, 21–2, 50–2, *52*, 53
Browning, Tod 85
Bruce, Lenny 25
Buffy the Vampire Slayer 33, 80
businessmen (as characters) 59–64

C

Campbell, Ramsey 78
'Carlton, Dr' (character) *124*, 124–5
Carmichael, Rodick 52–3
Carry on Girls (1973) 92
Carry on Screaming (1966) 75
Casablanca (1943) 33
catchphrase(s) 22, 84–5
The Catherine Tate Show 18
Catterick 24, 133
A Change of Sex 124
Chapman, Graham 6, 7, 25
'Charlie' (character) *90*, 90–2, *91*, 118, *119*
Chenery-Wickens, Diane 14

childlike qualities, as
  character trait 61–3
Children of the Stones 80
'Chinnery' (character) 67,
  68, 99–103
Christmas Special 77,
  79–80, 86–7, 88–104,
  129, 137*n*93
  DVD extras 137*n*93
  opening credits 88, *89*
  qualities 104
  'Solutions' (first story)
    89–92
  'The Vampire of
    Duisburg' (second
    story) 92–8
  'The Curse of Karrit
    Poor' (third story)
    99–103
Chuck, Charlie 21
The Cicerones 77–8, 133
Clark, Lawrence Gordon
  98
Cleese, John 6, 25, 105
Collins, Joan 138*n*119
The Comedians 53
The Comic Strip Presents
  18, 66, 67
Condon, Paul 16–17
Coogan, Steve 12, 21,
  76
Coogan's Run 12
Coronation Street 49
countryside, screen
  depictions
  as gruesome 64–5, 66
  as idyllic 66–7
  L of G's satire/perversion
    of 66–9
cross-dressing
  avoidance 115–16
  comic implications 31,
    57–8
cult TV/comedy
  defining characteristics
    16–17, 38

cult TV/comedy *cont.*
  examples 18–19
  'geography' 36
Cushing, Peter 76, 90

D

Daniels, Phil 55
'dark comedy',
  characteristics/
  examples 19, 24–33
Davis, Julia 24
Davison, Peter 67
Dawson, Les 50–2, 53,
  54, 57–8
The Day Today 21
Dead of Night 98
Dead Ringers 19
'Dean' (character) 126–7,
  127
Death in Venice (1971) 10
Deliverance (1972) 63
'Denton family' (characters)
  34, *35*, 45–6, *47*,
  69–72, *70*, *71*, *72*
Dickens, Charles 98
Doctor Who 4, 9, 67, 77,
  78, 80, 82, 132–3,
  134*n*3, 137*n*104
  'The Idiot's Lantern' 81
  'The Unquiet Dead' 102
Don't Look Now (1973)
  76
Douglas, Mary 71
*Dr Terrible's House of
  Horrible* 76, 77
Dr Terror's House of Horrors
  (1964) 76, 89–90,
  92–3
Dracula films 87–8, 94
DVDs 36
  commentary 36–8, 54
  extras 103, 137*n*93
  third series 105
Dyson, Jeremy 3, 20
  as actor 5, 76, 100,
    101, 121, 137*n*93

Dyson, Jeremy *cont.*
  comments:
  on bad taste 27–8,
    31
  on Christmas Special
    104
  on colleagues 5, 6, 9,
    12, 134*n*9
  on design 34
  on early career 8, 9,
    75
  on horror genre/
    influence 75, 99
  on murder 65
  on northern humour/
    ethos 49, 52
  on third series 105–6,
    107–8, 126
  on writing influences
    23
  creative input 5–6, 41
  DVD commentaries
    37–8, 75
  screen portrayal 132
  work outside *L of G* 24,
    77–8, 136*n*90
  writing methods/styles
    6–8

E

Early Doors 50
Eco, Umberto 33, 38
Edinburgh Festival 12
'Edward' (character) 64–6,
  83
  death 109, 131
Ekland, Britt 45
Elliott, Denholm 99
Emery, Dick 22
Enfield, Harry 42
'eternal triangle' storylines
  118
Ever Decreasing Circles
  58–9
Extras 105
Eyes Wide Shut (1999) 92

149

F

Families at War 22
fans 33–4, 36–7
'Farmer Tinsel' (character)
  68, 68–9
The Fast Show 17, 20,
  21, 22, 34, 39
Father Ted 59
Fawlty Towers 7, 18, 105,
  116
Fielding, Noel 20
Frank, Alan 78
Freud, Sigmund 82, 87,
  138*n*118
From beyond the Grave
  (1973) 76, 90–1
Fry, Stephen 18
The Full Monty (1997) 44
Funland 24, 133,
  139*n*159
Furness, Christine 115–16

G

Garth Marenghi's Dark Place
  77
Gatiss, Mark 6, 75, 122
  characters portrayed by
    3–4, 12, 31, 41, 76,
    103
  comments:
    on character popularity
      131
    on colleagues
      134*n*12, 138*n*117,
      139*n*159
    on horror/gothic 80,
      87–8, 99
    on offensive vocabulary
      32–3
    on pre-TV career 9,
      10–11, 14
    on third series 106,
      108
    on writing styles 6
  DVD commentaries/
    extras 37–8, 78,
    103, 105

Gatiss, Mark *cont.*
  early life 134*n*4
  work outside *L of G* 4,
    20–1, 24, 77–8, 81,
    102–3, 132–3,
    134*n*0, 137*n*104
  writing methods/styles
    6–8
'gender-bending' narratives
  111–15
  see also cross-dressing
The Generation Game 22
'Geoff' (character) 59–64,
  60, *62*, *63*, 118–19,
  120
  joke-telling/stand-up act
    60–1, 119–22,
    121–2
George and Mildred 57
Gervais, Ricky 18, 105,
  106
ghost stories, Victorian/TV
  traditions 98–9,
  101–2
  evoked by *L of G*
    99–103
The Ghosts of Motley Hall
  80
Gifford, Denis 78
Gilliam, Terry 16
Gimme Gimme Gimme 17,
  134*n*17
Girard, René 118
Godber, John 8
The Good Life 72
The Goodies 21
gothic tradition/elements
  75–104
  and the grotesque
    82–4
  and horror films 76
  and northern/rural
    settings 1, 66, 74
Graham, Alison 106–7
Grant, Julia (formerly
  George Roberts) 124

Griffths, Trevor, *Comedians*
  53
Grossman, Loyd 23
grotesque, elements in
  gothic/*L of G* 82–4,
  11/ 18
Guinness, Alec 11, 12
Gwenllian Jones, Sara 38

H

Hadfield, Derbys. 36, 48
Haig, David 122
Hammer Films 76
Hammer House of Horror
  (TV) 76
Hancock, Tony 7
Heartbeat 66
Heller, Joseph 24
'Herr Lipp' (character)
  31–2, *32*, *93–7*, 93–8
Herriot, James 66–7
Highgate House of Horror
  (home movie, 1995)
  76, 137*n*93
Higson, Andrew 49
Higson, Charlie 39
Hill, Benny 54
Hills, Matt 36
Hoggart, Richard 50, 54
Hope, Tim 34
Horner, Grenville 13, 34
horror genre
  cinematic traditions
    75–9
  and League's background
    75–6, 77–8
  referenced/parodied in
    L of G 66, 76,
    84–5, *86*, *87*, 88–9,
    89, 92–8
  TV expressions 79–81
Human Remains 24
*100 Greatest Scary
  Moments* 79–81
Hutchings, Peter 66, 76,
  83

I

Iannucci, Armando 21
Idle, Eric 7
I'm Alan Partridge 24
incest, (implied) depictions
    66
internet
    fansites/discussion
        groups 37, 88
    online reviews 107
'Iris' (character) 58, *59*,
    72–3, *73*
Izzard, Eddie 11

J

Jackanory 103
Jackson, Paul 49
Jacobs, W. W., *The
    Monkey's Paw* 99
Jam 24, 27–8, 30–1
James, M. R. 80–1, 98,
    103
Jones, Freddie 80
Jones, Terry 6, 16, 99,
    110, 129
'Judee Levinson' (character)
    70, 72–3, *73*

K

Kane, Sarah 13
Kaveney, Roz 36
Kay, Peter 23, 53
Keeping Up Appearances
    72
Keith, Sheila 77
Kes (1969) 81
The Killing of Sister George
    (1968) 111
King, Geoff 32
Kinski, Klaus 94
'Kitchen Sink' drama
    49–50, 59
Kitzmann, Rob 13
Kneale, Nigel 66, 98,
    138n124
Krzywinska, Tanya 117–18

L

'Lance' (character)
    111–15
Last of the Summer Wine
    36, 66
laugh track, use of 31, 86,
    107, 109
Laurie, Hugh 18
The League of Gentlemen
    (programme)
    casting 3–6, 21–2
    characterisation 1,
        3–4, 39–42, 54–74,
        115–18, 122–9 (*see
        also* businessmen;
        masculinity; women;
        names of characters)
    cinematography 42–4,
        44, 45, 49–50, *51*,
        95–6
    comic style 6–8
    costume/make-up 44–5
    critical/popular response
        1–2, 30, 105,
        106–7
    cult status 16, 18–21,
        38
    design 34–5, *35*
    generic characteristics
        1–2, 75–104
    genesis 9–15
    influences 6–7, 8, 12,
        22–4, 49–50, 75–9,
        129
    music 13–14, 109
    opening credits 43, 88
    ratings 17–18, 134n17
    'real-life' location 36
    real-life prototypes for
        characters 85,
        116–17
    referencing of film/TV
        standards *see* gothic;
        horror
    regional setting 1, 13,
        33–6, 48–54

*The League of Gentlemen
    cont.*
    storylines 45–6, 73–4
    vocabulary 32–3, 54
    writing process 6–8
    see also Christmas
        Special; *The Making
        of Series Three*;
        series three
'The League of Gentlemen'
    (writing/performing
    team)
    appearance/dress sense
        20
    commentary styles
        37–8
    naming 10–11
    post-*L of G* careers
        132–3
    regional origins 48
    screen portrayals
        131–2
    work before TV 9–15
    writing partnerships
        6–8, 106
    see also individual names
*The League of Gentlemen
    Are behind You* (stage)
    132
*The League of Gentlemen's
    Apocalypse* (2005)
    38, 131–2
Leigh, Mike 55
'Les McQueen' (character)
    34–5, *35*, *43*
Lewis, Nancy 20
Little Britain 2, 7, 13, 21,
    22
    comparisons with *L of G*
        19–20, 109, 132
'Local' comedy/ethos
    58–9, 64–6, 130
'local shop' setting 59,
    64–6, 76
Local Show for Local People
    (stage) 17–18

'Lonely Water' (public-
information film)
80–1
Lost 33
Lovell, Terry 49
Lucas, Matt 20

M
MacLean, Alistair 116
Maconie, Stuart 64
Mad magazine 25
Magpie 81
The Making of Series Three
33, 105–6
Manning, Bernard 53,
135*n*54
masculinity, treatments of
41–2, 59–64
The Matrix (1999) 21
'Mau Mau' sketch 7,
60–1
McLean, Gareth 86, 106
Meantime 55
Mellor, Kay 8
Melville, Andrew 93
Messingham, Simon
9–10
The Mighty Boosh 19, 20,
21, 34, 132
'Mike' (character) 59–64,
60, 62
Miller, Jonathan 98
Milligan, Spike 16
Mills, Brett 109
misogyny, allegations/
examples 54, 58
Mitchell, David 18
*Monty Python's Flying
Circus* 3, 5–6, 21,
129
comparisons with *L of G*
16–17, 18, 25, 28,
41, 52–3, 110
Morecambe, Eric 22
Morgan-Russell, Simon
49

Morris, Chris 11, 21, 24,
27–8
Mortimer, Bob 11, 21–2,
23–4
Muldoon, Roland 22–3
The Munsters 77
Murphy, Stuart 20
Mystery and Imagination
76

N
'Neds' (character) 127–8
Night of the Demon (1957)
44, 136–7*n*90
Nighty Night 12, 24
'northern' comedy,
ethos/examples 22–4,
48–54
'working man' traditions
50–3
'northern gothic,' critical
use of term 1
'nosebleed epidemic' storyline 46, 50
Nosferatu the Vampire
(1979) 94
nostalgia 82
Nuttall, Jeff 52–3

O
O'Brien, Richard 8
O'Donovan, Gerald 106,
111–15
The Office 18, 24, 105,
106–7
On the Hour (radio) 21
*On the Town with The
League of Gentlemen*
(radio) 12–13, 34,
39–41, 64, 69, 72,
118
Open All Hours 59
Orton, Joe 24, 25–6
Orwell, George 48, 56–7
'Owen' (character) 122–3,
123

P
Padbury, Wendy 78
Palin, Michael 6, 41, 99,
129
Palmer, Jerry 126–7
'Papa Lazarou' (character)
84–8, *86, 87*,
137*n*115
catchphrases 84–5,
87
in Christmas Special
86–7
critical response 106
first appearance 84–6
Papalazarou, Peter 85
Patton Walsh, Nick 106
Paul, William 83–4
'Pauline' (character) 54–6,
56, 115, *116, 125*
Peak Practice 36
Pemberton, Steve 75,
139*n*154
characters portrayed
3–4
DVD commentaries
37–8, 78
performance style 4
work outside *L of G*
133
writing methods/styles
6–8
Pertwee, Jon 80
Peter Kay's Phoenix Nights
24, 50, 53
Phillips, Daniel 14
Pinter, Harold 24
The Pipkins (TV) 138*n*127
Pleasence, Angela 91
Pleasence, Donald 80–1,
91
Plowman, Jon 14–15, 93
'Pop' (character) 41–2, *43*
Porter, Laraine 57–8
Psycho (1960) 95
Psychoville (projected)
133

Q

The Quatermass Experiment
66, 81, 137n104

R

The Railway Children
(1970) 103
Randall and Hopkirk
(Deceased) 24
Randle, Frank 53
realist drama, similarities
with/influences on L of
G 49–50, 59
Red Dwarf 17, 134n17
Reeves, Vic 11, 21–2,
23–4, 50–2
Rentaghost 80
Reservoir Dogs (1992) 44
Resident Evil 20
Ripping Yarns 41, 99, 129
Roberts, George see Grant,
Julia
Rock Profiles 20
Rodgers, Jemma 13, 93
Rohmer, Sax 77
Root, Jane 19
Rosengard, Peter 21
'Ross' (character) 55–6,
56, 115, 116, 126
Ross, Jonathan 23
Rossiter, Leonard 12
Routledge, Patricia 57
The Royle Ramily 13

S

Salem's Lot (TV) 138n124
The Same Dog (oratorio)
137n97
Sangster, Jim 16–17
Sconce, Jeffrey 81
Sedgwick, Eve Kosofsky
118
series three 105–30,
112–14
creative difficulties (and
video diary) 105–6

series three cont.
critical/popular reception
105, 106–7, 125–6
decision to make 105
new characters 122–9
participants' evaluation
105–6, 107–8
qualities/failings
108–9, 126–7
storylines 109–22,
139n147
see also The Making of
Series Three
Shearsmith, Reece 3, 54
characters portrayed
4–5, 88, 93,
138n123
DVD commentaries
37–8
performance style 4–5,
24, 53, 138n117
work outside L of G
20–1, 24, 133
writing methods/styles
6–8
Sheen, Michael 132
Shields, Rob 49
The Shining (1980) 21
Shipman, Harold 65,
124
Shooting Stars 22
The Signalman 98–9
Sim, Alastair 12
The Simpsons 137n94
The Smell of Reeves and
Mortimer 21–2, 23
Smith, Sarah 12–13
Something Wicked This Way
Comes (1983) 85
The South Bank Show 13
Spaced 20–1, 34
Spitting Image 13
Star Trek 33
Steig, Michael 83, 118
'Stella' (character) 56–7,
90–2, 91, 118

Steptoe and Son 7
The Stone Tape 98
Straw Dogs (1971) 66
'Stumphole Cavern' sketch
7, 26–7, 27
Styan, J. L. 25
suburbia, depictions/echoes
69–74
'Sunny' (character)
115–18
Sweet, Matthew 82

T

Talbot, Joby 13–14, 109,
137n97
Tales from the Crypt (1972)
138n119
Tales of the Unexpected
76
Talking Heads 26, 122
The Talmud 85
Tarantino, Quentin 20
Tarbuck, Liza 90
Tate, Catherine 7, 18, 22
Tekken 20
Thatcher,
Margaret/Thatcherite
ideology 55
Theatre of Blood (1973)
76
'thick text' 36–7
This Is It! (stage) 9–10,
85
Thomas, Mark 8
Thompson, Ben 5, 24,
125–6
Thompson, Mark 14
Tigon Films 76, 78
Timothy, Christopher 67
Tittybangbang 21, 132
Tobias, Oliver 77
Torchwood 66
Tovey, Roberta 78
'Tubbs' (character) 64–6,
67, 83, 136n78
death 109, 131

Twin Peaks 39
The Two Ronnies 22

V
Vaughan, Johnny 33
Vault of Horror (1973)
88–9, 92–3
Vault of Horror 35 (comic)
138n119
Vic Reeves' Big Night Out
21
The Vicar of Dibley 66
*Victoria Wood as Seen on
TV* 48
Victorian literature/
atmosphere *see* ghost
stories
Viner, Brian 30
'Vinnie'/'Reenie' (characters)
28–31, *29*
Viz (comic) 23, 65,
127
Vonnegut, Kurt 24

W
Walliams, David 20, 67
Walters, Julie 57
A Warning to the Curious
98
Webb, Robert 18
Welland, Colin 8
West, Fred/Rosemary 65
Wheatley, Helen 76, 79,
82, 98–9
Whistle and I'll Come to You
98
White, Vanessa 14
Whitehouse, Paul 39
The Wicker Man (1973) 11,
45, 64–5, 66, 76, 80
Wilmut, Roger 17, 21, 54,
105
Wise, Ernie 22
witches, treatment of 92,
92
The Wizard of Oz (1939)
80

The Woman in Black
138n124
women, characters 31,
54–9
background in 'northern
experience' 54
played by women
115–16
sexuality 57–8
as tyrants 54–6, 57
see also cross-dressing;
misogyny
Woo, John 21
Wood, Victoria 8, 48,
50–2, 54, 57, 77
Woodward, Edward 76
Wymark, Patrick 78

Y
The Young Ones 18,
126–7

Also Published

Buffy the Vampire Slayer	**Queer as Folk**
Anne Billson	Glyn Davis
Doctor Who	**Seinfeld**
Kim Newman	Nicholas Mirzoeff
Edge of Darkness	**Star Trek**
John Caughie	Ina Rae Hark
The Likely Lads	**Seven Up**
Phil Wickham	Stella Bruzzi
The Office	**The Singing Detective**
Ben Walters	Glen Creeber
Our Friends in the North	
Michael Eaton	